# OF MICE AND MEN

by John Steinbeck

Literature Guide Developed by Kristen Bowers
for *Secondary Solutions*®

ISBN-10: 0-9816243-3-2
ISBN-13: 978-0-9816243-3-4

© **2009 Secondary Solutions LLC. All rights reserved**.
A classroom teacher who has purchased this Guide may photocopy the materials in this publication for his/her classroom use only. Use or reproduction by a part of or an entire school or school system, by for-profit tutoring centers and like institutions, or for commercial sale, is strictly prohibited. No part of this publication may be reproduced, transmitted, translated or stored without the express written permission of the publisher. Created and printed in the United States of America.

THE *FIRST* SOLUTION FOR THE SECONDARY TEACHER®
WWW.4SECONDARYSOLUTIONS.COM

# *Of Mice and Men* Literature Guide

**About This Literature Guide** ............................................................................................ 4
**How to Use Our Literature Guides** ................................................................................... 5
**Sample Agenda and Teacher Notes** ................................................................................. 6
**Standards Focus: Elements of Fiction** ............................................................................. 9
**Standards Focus: Exploring Expository Writing** ............................................................ 10
   *Author Biography: John Steinbeck* ............................................................................. 10
      **Comprehension Check: Author Biography** ........................................................11
**Standards Focus: Historical Context** ............................................................................. 12
   *The Great Depression* .................................................................................................. 12
      **Comprehension Check: The Great Depression** .................................................13
   *Migrant Workers of California* ...................................................................................... 14
      **Comprehension Check: Migrant Workers of California** .....................................15
**Standards Focus: Elements of Fiction Activity** ............................................................. 16
**Standards Focus: Allusions and Terminology** .............................................................. 17
**Standards Focus: Idioms and Expressions** ................................................................... 20
**Vocabulary List** ................................................................................................................. 22
**Anticipation/Reaction Activity** ........................................................................................ 23
   *Pre-Reading Individual Reflection* .............................................................................. 24
   *Post-Reading Individual Reflection* ............................................................................ 24
**Standards Focus: Note-Taking and Summarizing** ........................................................ 25
   *Note-Taking and Summarizing Example* .................................................................... 26
**Chapter One** ...................................................................................................................... 27
   *Note-Taking and Summarizing* .................................................................................... 27
   *Comprehension Check* ................................................................................................ 28
   *Standards Focus: Dialogue* ......................................................................................... 29
   *Assessment Preparation: Word Analysis* ................................................................... 32
**Chapter Two** ...................................................................................................................... 37
   *Note-Taking and Summarizing* .................................................................................... 37
   *Comprehension Check* ................................................................................................ 38
   *Standards Focus: Analyzing Poetry* ........................................................................... 39
   *Assessment Preparation: Context Clues* ................................................................... 41
**Chapter Three** ................................................................................................................... 43
   *Note-Taking and Summarizing* .................................................................................... 43
   *Comprehension Check* ................................................................................................ 44
   *Standards Focus: Recognizing Vivid Details* ............................................................ 45
   *Assessment Preparation: Word Origins* .................................................................... 47
**Chapter Four** ..................................................................................................................... 50
   *Note-Taking and Summarizing* .................................................................................... 50
   *Comprehension Check* ................................................................................................ 51
   *Standards Focus: Conflict and Effect* ........................................................................ 52
   *Assessment Preparation: Word Roots* ...................................................................... 54
**Chapter Five** ..................................................................................................................... 57
   *Note-Taking and Summarizing* .................................................................................... 57
   *Comprehension Check* ................................................................................................ 58
   *Standards Focus: Characterization and Character Types* ...................................... 59
   *Assessment Preparation: Determining Parts of Speech* .......................................... 62
**Chapter Six** ....................................................................................................................... 65
   *Note-Taking and Summarizing* .................................................................................... 65
   *Comprehension Check* ................................................................................................ 66
   *Standards Focus: Theme* ............................................................................................ 67
   *Assessment Preparation: Determining Parts of Speech* .......................................... 69
**Quiz: Chapter One** ........................................................................................................... 72
**Vocabulary Quiz: Chapter One** ....................................................................................... 73
**Quiz: Chapter Two** ........................................................................................................... 74

**Vocabulary Quiz: Chapter Two** .................................................................................... **75**
**Quiz: Chapter Three** ............................................................................................... **76**
**Vocabulary Quiz: Chapter Three** ................................................................................. **77**
**Quiz: Chapter Four** ................................................................................................. **78**
**Vocabulary Quiz: Chapter Four** ................................................................................... **79**
**Quiz: Chapters Five and Six** ...................................................................................... **80**
**Vocabulary Quiz: Chapters Five and Six** ....................................................................... **81**
**Vocabulary Review: Chapters 1-3** ................................................................................ **82**
**Vocabulary Review: Chapters 4-6** ................................................................................ **83**
**Final Test** ............................................................................................................. **84**
**Final Test: Vocabulary** ............................................................................................. **87**
**Final Test: Multiple Choice** ....................................................................................... **90**
***Of Mice and Men* Teacher Guide** ............................................................................. **93**
   *Summary of the Novel* ........................................................................................... *93*
   *Vocabulary with Definitions* .................................................................................... *95*
   *Pre-Reading Activities* ........................................................................................... *97*
   *Post-Reading Activities and Alternative Assessment* ...................................................... *98*
   *Essay Ideas* ........................................................................................................ *100*
   *Writing Ideas* ..................................................................................................... *101*
   *Project Rubric A* ................................................................................................. *102*
   *Project Rubric B* ................................................................................................. *103*
   *Response to Literature Rubric* ............................................................................... *104*
**Answer Key** ........................................................................................................ **106**

## About This Literature Guide

**Secondary Solutions**® is the endeavor of a high school English teacher who could not seem to find appropriate materials to help her students master the necessary concepts at the secondary level. She grew tired of spending countless hours researching, creating, writing, and revising lesson plans, worksheets, quizzes, tests and extension activities to motivate and inspire her students, and at the same time, address those ominous content standards! Materials that were available were either juvenile in nature, skimpy in content, or were moderately engaging activities that did not come close to meeting the content standards on which her students were being tested. Frustrated and tired of trying to get by with inappropriate, inane lessons, she finally decided that if the right materials were going to be available to her and other teachers, she was going to have to make them herself! Mrs. Bowers set to work to create one of the most comprehensive and innovative Literature Guide sets on the market. Joined by a middle school teacher with 21 years of secondary school experience, **Secondary Solutions**® began, and has matured into a specialized team of intermediate and secondary teachers who have developed for you a set of materials unsurpassed by all others.

Before the innovation of **Secondary Solutions**®, materials that could be purchased offered a reproducible student workbook and a separate set of teacher materials at an additional cost. Other units provided the teacher with student materials only, and very often, the content standards were ignored. **Secondary Solutions**® provides all of the necessary materials for complete coverage of the literature units of study, including author biographies, pre-reading activities, numerous and varied vocabulary and comprehension activities, study-guide questions, graphic organizers, literary analysis and critical thinking activities, essay-writing ideas, extension activities, quizzes, unit tests, alternative assessment, online teacher assistance, and much, much more. Each Guide is designed to address the unique learning styles and comprehension levels of every student in your classroom. All materials are written and presented at the grade level of the learner, and include ***extensive coverage of the content standards.*** As an added bonus, all teacher materials are *included*!

As a busy teacher, you don't have time to waste reinventing the wheel. You want to get down to the business of *teaching*! With our professionally developed teacher-written literature Guides, **Secondary Solutions**® has provided you with the answer to your time management problems, while saving you hours of tedious and exhausting work. Our Guides will allow you to focus on the most important aspects of teaching—the personal, one-on-one, hands-on instruction you enjoy most—the reason you became a teacher in the first place.

# How to Use Our Literature Guides

Our Literature Guides are based upon the *National Council of the Teachers of English* and the *International Reading Association's* national English/Language Arts Curriculum and Content Area Standards. The materials we offer allow you to teach the love and full enjoyment of literature, while still addressing the concepts upon which your students are assessed.

Our Guides are designed to be used as standards-based lessons on particular concepts or skills. Guides may be used in their sequential entirety, or may be divided into separate parts. Not all activities must be used, but to achieve full comprehension and mastery of the skills involved, it is recommended that you utilize everything each Guide has to offer. Most importantly, you now have a variety of valuable materials to choose from, and you are not forced into extra work!

**There are several distinct categories within each Literature Guide:**
- ***Comprehension Check: Exploring Expository Writing***—Worksheets designed to address the exploration and analysis of functional and/or informational materials.
    - ✓ *Author Biography*
    - ✓ *Biographies of non-fiction characters*
    - ✓ *Relevant news and magazine articles, etc.*
- ***Comprehension Check***—Similar to *Exploring Expository Writing*, but designed for comprehension of narrative text—study questions designed to guide students *as they read the text*.
- ***Standards Focus***—Worksheets and activities that directly address the content standards and allow students extensive practice in literary skills and analysis. *Standards Focus* activities are found with every chapter or section. Some examples:
    - ✓ *Figurative Language*
    - ✓ *Irony*
    - ✓ *Flashback*
- ***Assessment Preparation***—Vocabulary activities which emulate the types of vocabulary/grammar proficiency on which students are tested in state and national assessments. *Assessment Preparation* activities are found within every chapter or section. Some examples:
    - ✓ *Context Clues*
    - ✓ *Connotation/Denotation*
    - ✓ *Word Roots*
- ***Quizzes and Tests***—Quizzes are included for each chapter or designated section; final tests as well as alternative assessment are available at the end of each Guide. These include:
    - ✓ *Multiple Choice*
    - ✓ *Matching*
    - ✓ *Short Response*
- ***Pre-Reading, Post-Reading Activities, Essay/Writing Ideas plus Sample Rubrics***—Each Guide also has its own unique pre-reading, post-reading and essay/writing ideas and alternative assessment activities.

Each Guide contains handouts and activities for varied levels of difficulty. We know that not all students are alike—nor are all teachers. We hope you can effectively utilize every aspect our Literature Guides have to offer—we want to make things easier on you! If you need additional assistance, please email us at info@4secondarysolutions.com. Thank you for choosing Secondary Solutions®

# Sample Agenda and Teacher Notes

Our Literature Guides are designed to be used in their sequential entirety or may be divided into separate parts. Not all activities must be used, but to achieve full comprehension and mastery of the skills involved, it is recommended that you utilize as much as you can in each Guide. Below is a sample unit plan integrating all aspects of this *Of Mice and Men Literature Guide*. This agenda assumes students have the time to read together as a class. It will need to be modified if you intend to have your students read at home or have them complete a combination of reading in class and at home.

*\*Before getting into this novel, you may want to have a discussion about the use of the word "nigger" in the classroom. Some students will be offended by the word. It is important that as a class, you decide on the level of use of the word, and whether or not the use of the word or a substitute such as "the n-word" is necessary or appropriate in reading aloud and in class and small group discussions.*

## Week One
**Day One:** Review literary terms by reviewing *Standards Focus: Elements of Fiction* (page 9). Read/discuss *Author Biography: John Steinbeck* (pages 10-11). Discuss Steinbeck's life and how it may have influenced his writing; introduce *Historical Context: The Great Depression* (pages 12-13). For more resources (including pictures, articles, etc) to supplement discussion about Steinbeck and The Great Depression, visit our website at www.4secondarysolutions.com/Of_Mice_and_Men/Recommended_Resources.
**Day Two:** Complete/discuss *Historical Context: Migrant Workers of California* (pages 14-15), answering questions and engaging in discussion or journaling or both.
**Day Three:** Begin discussing the themes of the novel by having students complete the *Anticipation/Reaction Activities* and *Pre-Reading Individual Reflection* (pages 23-24). Discuss responses as a class, including the implications of the novel, predicting what students think the novel will be about. (Collect papers and save for Post-Reading responses.
**Day Four:** Complete the *Standards Focus: Elements of Fiction Activity* (page 16). Continue discussing responses as a class, including the implications of the novel, predicting what they think the novel will be about and using vocabulary from the elements of fiction in your discussion. Continue introducing the themes of the novel through *Pre-Reading Activities* (page 97).
**Day Five:** Look over the *Allusions and Terminology* (pages 17-19), and *Idioms and Expressions* (pages 20-21), as well as the *Vocabulary List* (page 22) for reference. You may wish to give students the definitions for the words (*Vocabulary List with Definitions* available on pages 95-96), or have them use a dictionary to look them up. Let students know that these lists are there to help them during their reading so that they can understand everything they are unfamiliar with. They should refer to these often.

## Week Two
**Day One:** Introduce/explain use of *Note-Taking and Summarizing* Activity (pages 25-26). Begin reading the novel. Read as much as you deem useful for the class period. As students read, they should be actively completing their *Note-Taking and Summarizing* chart for Chapter One (page 27). Approximately 20 minutes before the end of class, have students begin answering the *Comprehension Check* questions (page 28). Have them finish reading Chapter One for homework if necessary, completing the *Note-Taking chart* and *Comprehension Check* questions as they read.
**Day Two:** Have students complete *Standards Focus: Dialogue* (pages 29-31).
**Day Three:** Explain and assign the *Assessment Preparation: Word Analysis* activity (pages 32-36).
**Day Four:** Give *Quiz: Chapter One* (page 72) and *Vocabulary Quiz: Chapter One* (page 73). Begin reading Chapter Two, completing the *Note-Taking* chart and *Comprehension Check* questions (pages 37-38) as they did for Chapter One.
**Day Five:** Finish reading Chapter Two, completing the *Note-Taking* chart and *Comprehension Check* questions. Complete *Standards Focus: Analyzing Poetry* (pages 39-40).

### Week Three
**Day One:** Complete *Assessment Preparation: Context Clues* (pages 41-42).
**Day Two:** Give *Quiz: Chapter Two* (page 74) and *Vocabulary Quiz: Chapter Two* (page 75). Begin reading Chapter Three, completing the *Note-Taking* chart and *Comprehension Check* questions (pages 43-44).
**Day Three:** Continue reading Chapter Three, completing the *Note-Taking* chart and *Comprehension Check* questions (pages 43-44).
**Day Four:** Complete *Standards Focus: Recognizing Vivid Details* (pages 45-46). Introduce *Assessment Preparation: Word Origins* (pages 47-49) for homework.
**Day Five:** Give *Quiz: Chapter Three* (page 76) and *Vocabulary Quiz: Chapter Three* (page 77). Begin reading Chapter Four, completing the *Note-Taking* chart and *Comprehension Check* questions (pages 50-51).

### Week Four
**Day One:** Continue reading Chapter Four, completing the *Note-Taking* chart and *Comprehension Check* questions (pages 50-51).
**Day Two:** Complete *Standards Focus: Conflict and Effect* (pages 52-53).
**Day Three:** Complete *Assessment Preparation: Word Roots* (pages 54-56).
**Day Four:** Give *Quiz: Chapter Four* (page 78) and *Vocabulary Quiz: Chapter Four* (page 79). Begin reading Chapter Five, completing the *Note-Taking* chart and *Comprehension Check* questions (pages 57-58).
**Day Five:** Continue reading Chapter Five, completing the *Note-Taking* chart and *Comprehension Check* questions (pages 57-58).

### Week Five
**Day One:** Complete *Standards Focus: Characterization and Character Types* (pages 59-61).
**Day Two:** Complete *Assessment Preparation: Determining Parts of Speech* (pages 62-64).
**Day Three:** Read Chapter Six, completing the *Note-Taking* chart and *Comprehension Check* questions (pages 65-66).
**Day Four:** Complete *Standards Focus: Theme* (pages 67-68).
**Day Five:** Complete *Assessment Preparation: Determining Parts of Speech* (pages 69-71).

### Week Six
**Day One:** Give *Quiz: Chapters Five and Six* (page 80) and *Vocabulary Quiz: Chapters Five and Six* (page 81).
**Day Two:** Review for Final Test. Choose your own method of review, and/or have students complete *Vocabulary Crosswords* (pages 82-83). You may choose to review for more than one day.
**Day Three:** Give either version of the *Final Test* (pages 84-86 or pages 90-92) as well as the optional Final Vocabulary Test (pages 87-89). Some alternates to these tests are a project from the *Post-Reading and Alternative Assessment* ideas (pages 98-99), an essay exam from the *Essay/Writing Ideas* (pages 100-101) or any combination of the three test types. Two different *Project Rubrics* are on pages 102-103; a *Response to Literature Essay Rubric* is on pages 104-105.
**Day Four:** If you intend to continue the study of the novel, *Post-Reading Activities and Alternative Assessment* ideas are on pages 98-99.
**Day Five:** Continue *Post Reading/Alternative Assessment* activities (pages 98-99).

## Notes for the Teacher

*As mentioned on page 5, not all activities and worksheets in this Guide must be used. They are here to help you so that you have some options to work with. Feel free to use all or only some of the worksheets and activities from this Guide. Here are a few notes about this Guide:*

1. Penguin Books, 1994 edition, was used in compiling this Literature Guide for *Of Mice and Men*.
2. For many of the vocabulary activities, a good dictionary with etymology is needed. Students should have access to a good dictionary in the classroom as well as at home. Students can also utilize sites such as *Dictionary.com* to complete their work.
3. Additional resources such as pictures, supplemental articles, graphs, charts, etc. are always helpful to pique students' interest in the novel. We have a list of links to recommended web resources on our website to access these materials. Please visit our website at www.4secondarysolutions.com/Of_Mice_and_Men/Recommended_Resources.
4. Both the *Note-Taking and Summarizing* activities and *Comprehension Check* questions are there to help your students get the most out of the novel. Depending upon your students and their needs, you may opt to have them only take notes, or only do the questions, or alternate between the two.
5. *Post-Reading Activities and Alternative Assessment* ideas are located on pages 98-99. Again, these are suggestions only. These project ideas can be used in addition to a written test, or in place of it. Project rubrics are located on pages 102-103. Please note that the rubrics are slightly different: *Project Rubric A* is recommended for projects that have a small written element that does NOT have to be researched. *Project Rubric B* is recommended for projects that include a research component in which sources must be cited.
6. *Essay/Writing* ideas are located on pages 100-101. Often, having students choose ONE topic from 2-3 essay topics that you have chosen ahead of time, in addition to their written test, works well. Many of these options can also work as a process essay during your teaching of *Of Mice and Men*.
7. Vocabulary tests and quizzes are optional. If you wish to give the Final Vocabulary Test, you should use pages with either version of the Final Test. (Please note: the Final Vocabulary Test does not include all of the vocabulary words presented in this Literature Guide. The words students are most likely to see again and use in the near future have been chosen for the test. You may choose to tell the students to study all vocabulary words for the test, or you may give them the list of test words ahead of time, since the number of words introduced in this Guide can be daunting to some students.)

Name _____   Period _____

# Standards Focus: Elements of Fiction

In the study of literature, it is important to remember that a story consists of several elements: plot, characters, setting, point of view, conflict, symbol, and theme. In the realm of fiction, the author can place an emphasis on any one or more of these elements, or conversely, de-emphasize any of these elements. For example, some authors may want the reader to focus on the plot, so the setting of the story may not be a major focus. It is important when analyzing a piece of literature that you look at all of the elements and how they work *together* to create an entire story.

- **Plot** - the related series of events that make up a story
    - Exposition - the beginning of a story in which the main characters, conflicts, and setting are introduced
    - Rising action - the action that takes place before the climax; the plot becomes more complicated, leading to the climax
    - Climax - the turning point of the story; emotional high point for the protagonist
    - Falling action - the action that takes place after the climax, leading to the resolution
    - Resolution - the end of a story; problems are solved, and characters' futures may be foreshadowed
- **Conflict** - the struggle(s) between opposing forces, usually characters
    - Internal conflict - a character's struggle with himself or his conscience
    - External conflict - a character's struggle with an outside force, such as another character, nature, or his environment
- **Characters** - the individuals involved (either directly or indirectly) in the action of the story
    - Protagonist - the central character in a story; struggles against the antagonist
    - Antagonist - the conflicting force against the protagonist; can be another character, a force of nature, or the protagonist struggling against himself
- **Setting** - the time and place, or where and when, the action occurs
    - Physical - the physical environment in which a story takes place; this includes the social and political environment
    - Chronological - the time in which a story takes place (includes the era, season, date, time of day, etc.)
- **Point of View** - the perspective from which a story is told
    - Narrator - the "voice" that tells a story; may or may not reflect the opinions and attitudes of the author himself
    - First person - a narrator who uses the first-person pronouns (I, me, my, myself, etc.) when telling the story; focuses on the thoughts, feelings, and opinions of a particular character
    - Third person limited - a narrator who uses the third-person perspective with the third person pronouns (he, she, it, they, etc.); observes the action as an outside observer, revealing the thoughts, feelings, and opinions of *only one* character
    - Third person omniscient - like third-person limited, the third-person omniscient narrator uses the third-person perspective with the third-person pronouns (he, she, it, they, etc.); this type of narrator observes the action as an outside observer, however, revealing the thoughts, feelings, and opinions of *several* characters
- **Theme** - the main idea behind a literary work; the message in the story

Name _____   Period _____

## Standards Focus: Exploring Expository Writing
*Author Biography: John Steinbeck*

John Ernst Steinbeck Jr. is considered one of the greatest American authors of all time. Famous for such works as *Tortilla Flat, Cannery Row, The Grapes of Wrath, East of Eden*, and *Of Mice and Men*, Steinbeck artfully created believable characters living real life, and in doing so, brilliantly captured the strength and determination of the human spirit.

Steinbeck was born February 27, 1902 in Salinas, California, the only son of John Ernst Steinbeck Sr. and Olive (Hamilton) Steinbeck. His father was the treasurer of Monterey County, and his mother was a public school teacher. He grew up in the vast agricultural heart of the Salinas Valley, about 25 miles off the Pacific Coast, which later became the setting for many of his novels.

Growing up an avid reader, Steinbeck was captivated by adventure stories such as Sir Thomas Malory's *Le Morte d'Arthur* (The Death of King Arthur). At age 14, he decided to become a writer, and spent hours in his bedroom writing stories and poems, and even attempting his own translation of Malory's famous novel.

Steinbeck entered Stanford University in 1919, enrolling in writing, literature and a few science courses. Never fully committed to the idea of college, Steinbeck occasionally took classes which interested him, but left in 1925 without ever receiving a degree. He then moved to New York, and worked several odd jobs, from newspaper reporter to construction worker. He returned to his native California two years later, where he worked as a caretaker for an estate and completed his first novel, *Cup of Gold*, in 1929.

While the novel *Cup of Gold* was never a significant financial or critical success, Steinbeck was able to afford to marry his first wife, Carol, in 1930. Finally settled, Steinbeck concentrated on his writing, and in 1935, published the very successful novel, *Tortilla Flat*. Based on the lives of California *paisanos* (people of Indian and Spanish descent), Steinbeck was able to capture the often bleak, yet painfully realistic side of human life—a side of life he was able to witness firsthand.

*Of Mice and Men*, published in 1937, and *The Grapes of Wrath*, published in 1939, were arguably Steinbeck's most famous and controversial novels. *Of Mice and Men* was originally conceived as a play, and after Steinbeck rewrote the novelette for the stage, it received the Drama Critics Circle Award in 1937, and was nominated for a Pulitzer Prize. *The Grapes of Wrath*, a gritty, candid illustration of the lives of farmers during the Depression, received harsh criticism. This criticism did not deter people from buying the book, however, and the novel eventually became a huge success, winning the Pulitzer Prize in 1940.

After his marriage began to crumble, Steinbeck decided to travel with respected friend Ed Ricketts, a marine biologist. *Sea of Cortez* (1941), and *The Forgotten*

**Name** _____  **Period** _____

*Village* (1941) were said to have been inspired by Ricketts and their travels together. He divorced Carol in 1943, and married his second wife, Gwendolyn, with whom he had two sons, Thomas and John. After another rocky marriage, they divorced in 1948, and in 1950 he married his third wife, Elaine Scott.

Severely criticized and equally celebrated, Steinbeck wrote 28 novels in all. His later works, *Cannery Row* (1945), *East of Eden* (1951), a semi-autobiographical piece, and *The Winter of Our Discontent* (1961), were a few of the most acclaimed novels of his later years. After receiving numerous nominations throughout the 1950s and 1960s, Steinbeck was finally awarded the Nobel Prize for Literature in 1962. Steinbeck died in New York, December 20, 1968, at the age of 66.

Steinbeck's empathy with life during the Depression and his ability to capture human existence in all of its harsh cruelty and captivating glory, made his novels a powerful platform for social and political issues and established Steinbeck as one of the most effective and brilliant writers of his time.

## Comprehension Check: Author Biography

*Directions: After reading the article on John Steinbeck, answer the following questions using complete sentences on a separate sheet of paper.*

1. Steinbeck wrote 28 novels in all. In the order in which they were published, list the names of the novels mentioned in the article.
2. Compare and contrast *Of Mice and Men* and *The Grapes of Wrath*, according to the information you are given in the article.
3. In one or two paragraphs, summarize Steinbeck's personal life, from his childhood to his death.
4. In your own words, describe the general qualities of Steinbeck's novels, according to the article. Why do you think his novels are still popular today?
5. If you were completing a research project on Steinbeck, what two research questions would you want to investigate further? Form two questions for your research. Why did you choose to find out more about these ideas?
6. Referring to the information in the article, draw a timeline of **ten** important milestones in Steinbeck's life. Be sure to include a brief description and dates for each event.

Name _____  Period _____

# Standards Focus: Historical Context
*The Great Depression*

One of the worst periods in United States history was a time called the Great Depression. The many theories about the specific causes of this era are debated, however the widespread poverty and social despair that resulted are **indisputable**.

from the *Migrant Mother* Collection
by Dorothea Lange

During the 1920s, America was experiencing a time of great prosperity and living a life of excess; people had a lot of money and weren't afraid to spend it on new inventions such as automobiles, refrigerators, and the radio. For the first time, people had credit cards, and were spending more than they made. Individuals were living life to the fullest, and the U.S. economy began to thrive at an **unprecedented** rate.

On October 24, 1929, a day that came to be called "Black Thursday," the stock market began to "crash." This meant that the value of money had lost its worth. Essentially, what someone could have bought with one dollar the day before now cost three to five dollars. Although President Herbert Hoover declared the economic collapse a "passing incident" a few days later, following "Black Tuesday" on October 29, the economy continued its downward spiral. Businesses could no longer afford to pay their workers and began laying off hundreds of thousands of people. Banks could not afford to give people their money, and were forced to declare **bankruptcy**. People's life savings suddenly disappeared, and as a result, people could not afford to pay their house payments or buy food, clothing, or other necessities.

Because people had no money, harvesting and manufacture of new crops and products slowed drastically. Since many had no money to buy food, production slowed, and even more people lost their jobs. By 1932, 30% (about 16-20 million people) of the American population was unemployed. Since people couldn't work, they couldn't pay their debts, and many were left homeless. When inflation (a rise in prices) hit, even more people were homeless and jobless, forced to beg, borrow, and steal food just to survive. Because the American people could no longer afford to spend money, the economy worsened.

In 1932, Democrat Franklin D. Roosevelt was elected President of the United States in the hopes he could turn the economy around and help those who were suffering. Despite changes such as the New Deal—which helped instill faith in the government by introducing new programs such as Social Security, unemployment insurance, and disability insurance—mass unemployment and economic **stagnation** continued for several years. The onset of World War II soon sparked the economy, as foreign

**Name** _____    **Period** _____

countries began buying from American producers. While the Great Depression officially ended after the United States entered World War II in 1941, the scars of extreme poverty and despair had left their mark, and the Great Depression continues to be viewed as one of the most difficult periods in U.S. history.

## Comprehension Check: The Great Depression

*Directions: After reading the article about the Great Depression, answer the following questions using complete sentences on a separate piece of paper.*

1. Define the following words from the article: indisputable, unprecedented, bankruptcy, stagnation.
2. Describe life in the United States before the depression.
3. Explain what happened on "Black Thursday." What happened to the value of money? How did this affect people in the U.S.?
4. Why did production of new crops and goods slow during this time?
5. Why didn't people just go to the bank and take out their money or apply for a loan from the bank?
6. Explain the "New Deal."
7. Because people did not have jobs, they were forced to move from place to place and pick up any work they could find in order to feed themselves and their families. Describe what you think life might have been like for those people who were homeless transients.
8. Why did the Great Depression finally end? Explain what contributed to its end and how these things helped bring this devastating era to a close.

Name _____    Period _____

# Standards Focus: Historical Context
*Migrant Workers of California*

In addition to the economic hardship felt by the impact of the stock market crash, another important event contributed to the devastation of the Great Depression: an event known as the *Dust Bowl*. The Dust Bowl got its name from the dust storms stirred from the top soil following an immense drought across the United States. The areas hit hardest by the drought—Kansas, Oklahoma, Arkansas, and parts of Colorado and Texas—were devastated, as farms and crops and ultimately farmers' **livelihoods** were totally destroyed. Because so many farmers lost everything they had, they decided to try to find a better place to live. Many farmers decided to head west, to California, Oregon, and Washington.

"Okies" (people from Oklahoma) on Route 66 to California. (Farm Security Administration: Circa 1935)

During the 1920s, California became a tropical oasis, as it was heralded as an agricultural **mecca**. California had once touted itself as a state with a perfect climate for agriculture with plenty of jobs in the industry. Thousands of those forced out by the Dust Bowl flocked to California, and the state became overwhelmed with people looking to restart their lives. These people were not only farmers, but others such as retailers and those whose income relied on farm communities. Such people became known as ***migrant** workers*, since they would travel from place to place looking for jobs. There was work available for some, and many were able to start over in California. However, there were not enough jobs for everyone, and many people found themselves jobless and homeless.

Since so many migrant workers found themselves without work, they traveled wherever they could to find a job, often riding trains illegally, traveling from camp to camp with other homeless migrant workers. These camps became known as "squatter camps," "shack towns," or "Hoovervilles," named after President Herbert Hoover, who many disgruntled Americans blamed for the problems leading up to the Depression. These temporary camps were usually set up by rivers or streams and provided little shelter—usually a tent or shack. There were no toilets or showers, and the little food they had was cooked over an open campfire. According to a report of the National Labor Board in 1934, "we found filth, **squalor**, an entire absence of sanitation, and a crowding of human beings into totally inadequate tents or crude structures built of boards, weeds, and anything that was found at hand to give a pitiful **semblance** of a home at its worst. Words cannot describe some of the conditions we saw. During the warm weather, when the temperature rises considerably above 100 degrees, the flies and insects become a pest, the children are fretful, the attitude of some of the parents can be imagined, and innumerable

**Name** _____ **Period** _____

inconveniences add to the general discomfort. In this environment there is bred a social **sullenness** that is to be deplored, but which can be understood by those who have viewed the scenes that violate all the recognized standards of living."

Some farmers attempted to help more permanent workers by allowing them to live on the land on which they worked. Government agencies also tried to help the situation by setting up camps run by the people living there. Facilities such as toilets, showers, and washing machines were available at these camps. Relief in the form of money (often less than $40 per month per family) and food was made available to those who had been in California more than three years, but those who had been in California less than three years were left helpless. Still, those who received aid had to wait in long lines and since there were so many who needed help, many were turned away once food rations were gone.

When workers were able to work, the competition was fierce and the conditions were poor. A report from Alameda County in 1936 described these circumstances: "At one ranch 150 to 200 persons, Mexicans, Americans, high school boys, some families; reported at 6:30 in the morning, waited under the trees for call, some waited all day and were not called at all, others would work two hours and then check out, waiting until another truck was available, which again brings up the question of duration of employment. Twenty-five cents an hour is the scale, yet a person may only work four hours out of the twelve, but they must spend the rest of the time waiting in the hot sun or under the trees, subject to call of the foreman. It is certainly an unsatisfactory situation…"

Hope eventually came in the form of the New Deal and the creation of the Works Progress Administration, which provided thousands of jobs across the country. The program put many to work building government buildings, transportation systems, and projects including those in the arts, media, and literacy.

## Comprehension Check: Migrant Workers of California

*Directions*: After reading the article about Migrant Workers of California, answer the following questions using complete sentences on a separate piece of paper.

1. Use a dictionary to define the following words: livelihood, mecca, migrant, squalor, semblance, sullenness.
2. Why did so many farmers decide to migrate to the west?
3. What is a migrant worker?
4. Using your own words, describe the living conditions of many migrant workers.
5. Why are there quotation marks around part of the 3rd paragraph?
6. What kind of help was offered to the migrant workers?
7. Why did the migrant workers face competition for jobs? What did they have to do in order to get a job? How much might they get paid for their work?
8. What type of work did the Works Progress Administration provide?

Name _____  Period _____

# Standards Focus: Elements of Fiction Activity

Now that you are familiar with the elements of fiction and some of the historical context of the novel you are about to read, complete the activity below.

***Directions***: *Complete the chart below with predictions about the novel Of Mice and Men. Remember, these are predictions, so there really are no wrong answers, however, you must use the knowledge you gained from the pre-reading articles to help you. Be sure to answer ALL the questions posed to you. An example has been done for you.*

| | |
|---|---|
| **Plot**: Based upon your readings, what do you predict the novel will be about? Give a 3-5 sentence summary of your prediction. | |
| **Conflict**: What kinds of conflicts might the characters face? Include one internal conflict and one external conflict that one of the characters may face in the novel. | |
| **Characters:** What types of characters do you think you will read about in this story? What kinds of people do you think they will be? What do you think they might do for a living? | |
| **Setting**: Where and when do you think the story might take place? Be sure to include the physical environment of the story. | *Since we have read so much about California and Great Depression of the 1930s, I am predicting the novel will take place in California in 1935. Since it will take place in California in 1935, conditions will be harsh because of the Great Depression—work will be hard to find, money will be tight, and the characters will be depressed and face many challenges.* |
| **Theme:** What kids of themes do you predict will be presented in this novel? Write out 3-5 themes in complete sentence form. | |

Name _____  Period _____

# Standards Focus: Allusions and Terminology

**Chapter One**
1. **Soledad**: a city in Monterey County, California
2. **Salinas River**: the largest river of the central coast of California
3. **Gabilan mountains**: mountain range located on California's Central Coast along the Monterey County and San Benito County line
4. **sycamore**: a type of tree found in California, with large leaves and speckled brown and white bark
5. **tramps**: homeless people, often looking for work
6. **stilted heron**: a freshwater bird with a long neck and crested head
7. **bindle**: a bundle of personal belongings; a knapsack
8. **Howard Street**: Howard Street in San Francisco in Northern California; the two men may have stopped in San Francisco to look for work
9. **work cards**: an identity card indicating that a person is legally able to do work
10. **bus tickets**: a ticket that allowed a person to ride the bus
11. **Weed**: A mining town in Northern California, near Mt. Shasta
12. **periscope**: a long tubular instrument, usually on a submarine, that allows a viewer to see objects above the water
13. **thrashin' (threshing) machines**: machines for separating grain crops into grain or seeds and straw
14. **grain bags**: bags that hold seed for grain; usually worn over the shoulder
15. **supper**: a light meal eaten in the evening
16. **carp**: a large freshwater fish
17. **willow cotton**: a willow is a tree with long flexible branches; "willow cotton" is referring to the small flowers the tree bears
18. **stake**: an amount of money, usually enough to risk gambling
19. **brush**: a dense undergrowth of trees and bushes

**Chapter Two**
1. **bunks**: beds
2. **burlap ticking**: the "tick" is the outer fabric covering of a mattress; in this case the tick is made of burlap, a coarse but sturdy cloth
3. **apple box**: a sturdy wooden box used to store apples before going to market
4. **talcum powder**: a fine, perfumed powder used to absorb moisture on the skin
5. **Western magazines**: magazines full of cowboy stories and tales of the "Old West"
6. **cast-iron stove**: a wood- or fuel-burning stove designed to heat large spaces
7. **stovepipe**: a pipe used as a chimney for a fuel-burning stove
8. **scourges**: causes of widespread devastation such as disease or war
9. **swamper**: a handyman or person who handles odd jobs
10. **blacksmith**: someone who makes and repairs iron and metal objects such as horseshoes
11. **graybacks**: lice
12. **tick**: the outer fabric of a mattress; can refer also to the mattress itself
13. **liniment**: a liquid or cream applied to the skin as a pain reliever
14. **stable buck**: a man who works in a stable, usually feeding and taking care of horses
15. **skinner**: the head driver of animals, usually cattle, mules, or oxen
16. **Stetson hat**: a brand of cowboy hat manufactured by the John B. Stetson company
17. **spurs**: a small spike or spiked wheel attached to the heel of a rider's boot, used to get a horse to move faster
18. **bale**: a large bundle or package

Name _____ Period _____

19. **cesspool**: a covered underground tank or well for the collection of sewage
20. **drag-footed sheep dog**: a sheep dog is a type of dog bred to herd sheep; "dragfooted" means he is very old and moves very slowly and with some trouble
21. **muzzle**: an animal's nose and jaw
22. **Vaseline**: a type of petroleum jelly used to soften the skin
23. **patent medicine**: a medicine in which its contents are not completely disclosed; often these medicines claim to be "miracle cures"
24. **solitaire**: a card game for one person
25. **jerkline skinner**: the main driver of a mule team
26. **mules**: cross between a donkey and a horse
27. **poke**: a small bag or sack
28. **American River**: a river in California where gold was found in 1848, leading to the California Gold Rush
29. **pan gold**: look for gold; originally done using a metal pan for sifting
30. **wheeler**: a draft animal (such as a mule or horse) in a position closest to the wheels of the wagon
31. **bull whip**: a whip used to keep animals in line
32. **temple dancers**: women who perform sacred dances to express worship to their gods
33. **punks**: worthless, lazy young men
34. **blue ball**: in the game of snooker (similar to pool), the blue ball sits at the very center of the table; as the ball is pocketed, the player gets 5 points
35. **bitch**: a female dog
36. **shepherds**: a type of dog bred to herd sheep
37. **triangle**: an instrument made of metal in the shape of a triangle, used to call workers to a meal

**Chapter Three**
1. **horseshoe game**: an outdoor competition in which players attempt to throw a horseshoe around a stake in the ground
2. **Auburn**: a city located northeast of Sacramento and southwest of Lake Tahoe, California
3. **irrigation ditch**: a ditch to artificially supply dry land with water
4. **slug**: a shot; small drink
5. **rheumatism**: a condition causing inflammation and pain in muscles or joints
6. **Airedale**: a terrier dog breed from Yorkshire, England
7. **pulp magazine**: inexpensive fiction magazines published from the 1920s to the 1950s; named after the cheap wood pulp paper on which they were printed
8. **Peter Rand**: possibly a fictional writer of short stories for pulp magazines
9. **Dark Rider**: unknown story from pulp magazine
10. **cultivator**: a farm implement for stirring and pulverizing soil
11. **Luger pistol**: toggle locked, recoil operated, semi-automatic pistol
12. **leather thong**: a braided leather whip
13. **euchre**: a card game in which each player is dealt five cards and the player making trump must take three tricks to win the hand
14. **drawers**: pants
15. **Susy's place**: a house of prostitution
16. **shot**: a small amount of alcohol
17. **rag rug**: a rug constructed of narrow scraps of fabric
18. **kewpie doll**: a small, chubby doll with a tuft of hair on the top of her head
19. **phonograph**: a term for the first record players
20. **Golden Gloves**: the name given to annual competitions for amateur boxing in the United States
21. **whore house**: a house of prostitution
22. **hoosegow**: jail

Name _____    Period _____

23. **hot cakes**: another name for pancakes
24. **San Quentin**: the oldest prison in California, built in 1852
25. **win'mill (windmill)**: a device for harnessing wind power
26. **chicken run**: an enclosed yard for keeping poultry
27. **alfalfa**: a plant of the pea family, often used for livestock feed
28. **hutches**: small shelters, usually constructed from wire and wood, for keeping small animals such as rabbits
29. **setter dog**: a type of gundog used for hunting game
30. **bunk houses**: living quarters
31. **carnival**: a public festive occasion, often with costumes, music, dancing, rides, and sideshows
32. **circus**: a group of traveling entertainers, including clowns, acrobats, and sometimes animal trainers and their animals
33. **ball game**: refers to a baseball or football game
34. **welter (welterweight)**: a boxer weighing more than 135 pounds but less than 147
35. **terrier**: a dog of any one of many breeds of terrier type, which are typically small, wiry, very active and fearless dogs

**Chapter Four**
1. **harness**: a set of leather straps fitted to an animal so it can be controlled
2. **riveter**: a worker or machine that joins metal plates together
3. **hame**: a curved bar for controlling a draft animal
4. **trace chain**: a length of metal chain
5. **saddle soap**: a compound used to clean leather

6. **spectacles**: an early term for eye glasses
7. **nail keg**: a barrel or other container for holding nails
8. **rummy**: a card game in which players try for sequential cards
9. **manure pile**: a pile of horse excrement
10. **blackjack**: a card game in which the players seek to make a total closest to, but not more than, 21

**Chapter Five**
1. **Jackson fork**: a large mechanical hay fork, used for lifting large amounts of hay
2. **pulley**: a mounted wheel with a belt or chain that can change the direction of a pulling force
3. **mangers**: troughs from which livestock eat
4. **mules**: slipper-like shoes
5. **Riverside Dance Palace**: a fictional dance hall, which was a popular form of socialization for young men and women
6. **Hollywood**: Hollywood, California; known as the capital for movie-making
7. **silk**: a fine fiber made from the secretions of silkworms
8. **velvet**: a cotton, silk, or nylon fabric with a soft lustrous touch
9. **dugs**: the teats, udders, or breasts of a female animal

**Chapter Six**
1. **bull's-eye glasses**: glasses with thick convex lenses
2. **gingham apron**: an apron made from gingham, a checked cotton fabric
3. **snooker**: similar to pool, played with 15 red balls and 6 balls of various colors

Name _____    Period _____

# Standards Focus: Idioms and Expressions

**Chapter One**
1. 'coons: slang for raccoons, medium-sized mammals native to North America
2. jungle-up: at this time, a "jungle" was an area off the road where homeless people would camp; to "jungle-up" means to set up camp
3. "watchin' that blackboard": during this time, employment agencies would post any jobs available on a blackboard in front of their offices
4. "leave me have it": let me have it
5. "bucking": the process of harvesting
6. "bustin' a gut": working really hard
7. "puttin' nothing over": tricking
8. "sock you": punch you
9. "ain't fresh": is not sanitary or healthy
10. "in hot water": in trouble
11. "get a kick outta that": really like that
12. "poundin' their tail": working really hard
13. "blowin' our jack": wasting our money
14. "live off the fatta the lan'": live off the profits provided by selling crops
15. cream is so thick "you can hardly cut it": milk that is left sitting will separate, making a thick cream at the top

**Chapter Two**
1. "sore as hell": really angry
2. "pants rabbits": slang for crabs, a species of invertebrates that infest the pelvic region
3. "I ain't got the poop no more": "I don't have the energy anymore"
4. "gave us a bum steer": led in the wrong direction
5. "strong as a bull": extremely strong
6. "What you sellin'?": "What antics are you trying to pull?"
7. "flapper": mouth
8. "old man": father
9. "got on his shoulder": similar "chip on his shoulder", which means something bothering him; angry about something
10. "picking scraps": starting fights
11. "game guy": competitive person
12. "licks him": fights him and wins
13. "purty": pretty
14. "She got the eye": "She's a flirt."
15. "give…the eye": flirt
16. "pants is full of ants": jumpy and nervous
17. "tart": a prostitute or promiscuous woman
18. "get the can": get fired
19. "let 'im have it": fight back
20. "clear out": leave; move out
21. jail bait: a derogatory term for a young girl who is perceived as trying to sleep with an older man
22. "leave her be": leave her alone
23. rattrap: a trap for rats; in this case, Curley's wife is a trap for men
24. "eatin' raw eggs": some people believed that eating raw eggs could increase a man's strength and sexual stamina
25. "bits": slang for "cents"
26. "shove out of here": leave
27. "hit a pocket": get lucky
28. "slang": gave birth to
29. "in heat": in a sexually receptive state
30. "tangle with": fight with

**Chapter Three**
1. cuckoo: a derogatory name for someone, like calling someone "crazy"; also a family of medium-sized, slender birds
2. "fifty and found": fifty dollars plus additional amenities, such as a sleeping room and meals
3. "clean forgot": outright forgot
4. "rabbits an' tells the law": runs away quickly and tells the police
5. "scrammed outta there": ran away as quickly as possible
6. "gut ache": stomach ache

**Name** _____   **Period** _____

7. cripple: a derogatory term for someone who is physically impaired in some way
8. "whing-ding": a great writer; the best
9. "turning his hand": doing any work
10. looloo: a good-looking girl
11. yella-jackets: "yellow jackets"—a common name for wasps in North America
12. flop: intercourse with a prostitute
13. "walkin' bow legged": Whit is referring to a man contracting a venereal disease from one of the prostitutes from Clara's place
14. goo-goos: used to mean someone who is love-struck; a romantic
15. "see the fuss if it comes off": see the fight if it happens
16. Jap: a derogatory term for a Japanese person
17. "flat bust": completely poor
18. "swing her": make it happen
19. "swamp out": clean and take care of
20. "sling": throw
21. "bind her": satisfy her
22. "lay offa me": leave me alone
23. "yella as a frog belly": a coward
24. "like a fish on a line": squirming like a fish that has been caught

**Chapter Four**
1. "crazy as a wedge": mentally unstable
2. colored: an antiquated term for African-Americans
3. "took a powder": left in a hurry
4. booby hatch: insane asylum
5. "take you out in a box": remove your dead body in a coffin
6. twicet: a Southern term for "twice"

7. "bindle bums": lazy migrants
8. floozy: another word for "prostitute"
9. "two-bit": two cents; cheap
10. "two shots of corn": two shots of corn whiskey
11. "roll your hoop": reference to a game played by children in which they roll a large hoop, trying to keep it from falling
12. trap: mouth
13. "strung up on a tree": hung from a tree
14. "got it doped out": got it worked out; figured out

**Chapter Five**
1. "sonny boy": slang term for "young man"
2. "tenement" (tournament): game
3. "pitchers" (pictures): movies
4. "ol' lady": wife or mother
5. "fella": fellow
6. "previews": movie openings
7. "'an spoke on the radio": radio was the major form of entertainment and news at the time; radio programs would interview celebrities before a movie premiere
8. "ringer": an expert

**Chapter Six**
1. "sonofabitching": similar to "damn"
2. "stew the b'Jesus outta": bother
3. "greased jack-pin": a jackhammer
4. "blow it in": waste it
5. "hoot in hell": darn
6. "eatin'": bothering

Name _____  Period _____

# *Of Mice and Men*
# Vocabulary List

***Directions***: Use a dictionary to look up the following vocabulary words from the novel. Be sure to keep your definitions for use with future vocabulary worksheets and activities.

**Chapter One**
junctures
debris
mottled
recumbent
morosely
lumbered
brusquely
pantomime
contemplated
imperiously
anguished
yammered

**Chapter Two**
scoff (at)
mollified
pugnacious
gingerly
handy
ominously
slough
derogatory
flounced
plaintively
decisive
complacently

**Chapter Three**
derision
lynch
concealing
stride
gnawing
entranced
reprehensible
bemused
cowering
regarded
wryly
solemnly

**Chapter Four**
mauled
aloof
meager
liniment
fawning
disarming
scornful
brutally
indignation
averted
appraised
crestfallen

**Chapter Five**
jeering
hurled
sullenly
woe
consoled
contorted
writhed
muffled
bewildered
pawed
cringed
sniveled

**Chapter Six**
lanced
scudded
disapprovingly
haunches
retorted
belligerently
woodenly
monotonous
craftily
triumph
dutifully
jarred

Name _____     Period _____

# Anticipation/Reaction Activity

***Directions—Before reading the novel***: In the "Before Reading" column, write "yes" if you agree with the statement, "no" if you disagree with the statement, and "?" if you don't have a strong opinion or are not sure about the statement.

| Yes = I agree | No = I disagree | ? = I don't know |

| *Before Reading* | Statement | *After Reading* |
|---|---|---|
|  | 1) Having friends and a stable home fulfills two of our basic human needs. |  |
|  | 2) Mentally impaired people don't understand things and cannot function like "regular" people. |  |
|  | 3) People who are strong know their strength, and how much they can hurt other people if they want to. |  |
|  | 4) It is unnatural for people to have an attachment to, or feelings for, an animal. |  |
|  | 5) The purpose of life is to strive for, and eventually reach, our goals and dreams for the future. |  |
|  | 6) Killing another human being is intolerable, and should be punished. |  |
|  | 7) Running away from a crime is never acceptable. |  |
|  | 8) It is important for people to have a place where they feel like they belong. |  |

After completing the "Before Reading" column, get into small groups, then tally the number of "yes", "no," and "?" responses for each question. Each group member should keep track of the tally.

Group Members: _____

| Statement # | Yes | No | I Don't Know |
|---|---|---|---|
| 1 |  |  |  |
| 2 |  |  |  |
| 3 |  |  |  |
| 4 |  |  |  |
| 5 |  |  |  |
| 6 |  |  |  |
| 7 |  |  |  |
| 8 |  |  |  |

Once you have collected your data, discuss those issues about which your group was divided. Make your case for your opinions, and pay attention to your classmates' arguments. Once you have discussed all of the issues, answer the Pre-Reading Individual Reflection questions on the next page on your own.

*Your teacher will collect and keep your chart and responses to use after you have finished reading the novel, when you will complete the Post-Reading Individual Reflection.*

Name _____    Period _____

# Anticipation/Reaction Activity

## *Pre-Reading Individual Reflection*

**Directions**: *Use the information and discussion from the "Before Reading" responses to answer the following questions on a separate piece of paper. Be sure to use complete sentences.*

1. Which statements triggered the most thought-provoking or interesting discussion?
2. Summarize the discussion/debate.
3. For any of the statements that you discussed, what were some of the strongest or most memorable points made by your group members?
4. What was your reaction when a group member disagreed with the way you feel about an issue?
5. Was any argument strong enough to make you change your mind or want to change any of your initial responses? Why or why not? What made the argument effective?

## *Post-Reading Individual Reflection*

**Directions**: *After reading the novel, revisit your Anticipation/Reaction Activity and your answers to the discussion questions. Now that you have read the novel, complete the "After Reading" column on page 23 and answer the following questions on a separate piece of paper, comparing your responses. Answer each question using complete sentences.*

1. How many of your responses have changed since reading the novel?
2. Which statements do you see differently after reading the novel?
3. Describe an important part of the novel that affected you, or made you think differently after reading.
4. In small groups, talk to some of your classmates about their responses. How are their responses different after reading the novel?
5. Overall, are the feelings of your other group members the same or different from yours? Do any of their responses surprise you? Which ones? How?
6. Why do you think there might be so many different opinions and viewpoints? What do you feel has contributed to the way you and your other classmates responded to each statement?

Name _____    Period _____

# Standards Focus: Note-Taking and Summarizing

For some students, reading can be a difficult, tedious task. Part of the problem is that many students do not have the tools to read for meaning, and become disinterested because they cannot follow the action or do not understand, or cannot relate to, the events or the characters. To develop good reading habits, there are a few steps that you can take which will help you to understand and appreciate what you are reading.

- ❖ **As you read** each chapter of *Of Mice and Men:*

    - **Question**—*Ask yourself,* where is this story or scene, etc. taking place? What has happened before this? Who are the people involved? What do I not understand? What do I need to reread? What do I need my teacher to clarify? Do the Comprehension Check questions or answers leave you with more questions or problems you need to clarify? Use this section to ask those questions.
    - **Connect**—*Try to relate to the events or characters* in what you are reading. Has this or something like this ever happened to you? How did you handle this situation? Have you ever known a person like any of the characters? What other situations come to mind when reading? Why? Are there any lessons or themes you have seen before?

- ❖ **After you read** each chapter of *Of Mice and Men:*

    - **Comprehension Check Notes**—*Use this space to write notes* about what you would like to remember from the Comprehension Check questions for each section (things you might be quizzed on).
    - **Summarize**—*Break down* the most important information, details, or events of the story. Retell the events of the story in your own words.
    - **Predict**—*Try to make a guess or prediction* as to what may happen next in the novel. This will help you to stay focused on what you read next, as you try to unravel the story. What will happen next? What effect will this event have on those involved?
    - **Reflect**—*Think about why* you are reading the story. What do you think is the theme? What have you learned so far? Why are you reading this particular text in school? Do you like the story? Why or why not? Would you want to read or learn more about this author/genre/topic? Why or why not?

To help you become a more successful, active reader, you will be completing an activity like this for each chapter of *Of Mice and Men*. Each activity is designed to help you understand the action, conflict, and characters involved in the story, and to eventually appreciate the author's reasons for writing the novel. On the next page is a sample of the chart you will be completing, along with hints to help you complete each section.

Name _____  Period _____

## *Note-Taking and Summarizing Example*

| | |
|---|---|
| **Question** | In this space, write the names of the people involved, as well as where and when the story is taking place. Next, write down questions you have about the novel, and any questions about the reading that you do not understand and/or would like your teacher to clarify. Do the Comprehension Check questions or answers leave you with more questions or problems you need to clarify? |
| **Connect** | In this space, write down anything that you find familiar: either a situation you have experienced, a character that reminds you of someone, or an event from the story that is similar to something you have already read. |
| **Comprehension Check Notes** | Use this space to write anything you feel is important to remember from the Comprehension Check questions for each chapter. |
| **Summarize** | Retell, in your own words, the action and important details of your reading. Your summary should not be more than about one paragraph, or 5-7 sentences long. |
| **Predict** | In this space, write your prediction of what you think will happen next. What effect will this event have on those involved? |
| **Reflect** | In this space, write down any quotes, sayings, or moments that affect you in some way. So far, what do you think is the reason the author wrote this novel? Are there any themes you recognize? Do you like the novel so far? Why or why not? What changes could be made so that you understand or connect with the novel better? What else would you like to learn about this author/genre/topic? |

Name _____  Period _____

# Chapter One
*Note-Taking and Summarizing*

| | |
|---|---|
| **Question** | |
| **Connect** | |
| **Comprehension Check Notes** | |
| **Summarize** | |
| **Predict** | |
| **Reflect** | |

Name _____     Period _____

# Chapter One
*Comprehension Check*

***Directions****: To give you a comprehensive understanding of all aspects of the novel, answer the following questions using complete sentences on a separate sheet of paper. Be sure to use your Note-Taking chart to keep important notes for each chapter and to help you answer the Comprehension Check questions.*

1. Describe the two men. How are they different physically? How are they different mentally?
2. Why doesn't George want Lennie to drink the water?
3. Why does Lennie have a dead mouse in his pocket?
4. To where are George and Lennie headed?
5. Where are George and Lennie coming from?
6. What is your impression of the relationship between the two men? Why do you think George takes care of Lennie?
7. What does George tell Lennie to do when they get to where they are going?
8. When Lennie goes out to get wood for a fire, what does he bring back?
9. Who used to give Lennie mice? Why did she stop?
10. How is George resentful of Lennie? What does George wish he could do?
11. What dream do George and Lennie share?
12. Why do George and Lennie feel they are different from other men?
13. Where does George tell Lennie to go if he gets in trouble? Why do you think George makes it a point to be sure Lennie understands this?
14. Despite being slow, Lennie knows how to make George feel guilty. Describe two situations in which Lennie manipulates George and makes him feel bad. What does this reveal about their relationship?
15. You may have noticed that Steinbeck uses a lot of slang—even some curse words and foul language. Why do you think Steinbeck does this? What effect does the use of this language have on the way the story is told? How might the story be different if Steinbeck avoided this technique?

Name _____   Period _____

# Chapter One
*Standards Focus: Dialogue*

One of the unique aspects of **Of Mice and Men** is the use of dialogue. **Dialogue** *is a conversation between two or more characters, distinguished by the use of quotation marks. Since this novel was conceived by Steinbeck as a "playable novel," dialogue, rather than lengthy descriptive narration, helps the reader to understand the characters and plot. In drama, it is the actions and dialogue of the characters that tell the story. Dialogue can serve many different purposes. Dialogue:*

- develops characters as the reader is able to experience the character's own words. The way a person speaks, and how they say what they say, can reveal a lot about a person
- creates the setting through regional characteristics, such as dialects and slang, and helps to show how the characters live within their environment
- reveals important information about the plot and conflicts, without disturbing the momentum of the storyline
- allows the reader to experience the action as the character is experiencing it, rather than having it communicated from another perspective
- generates an impression of reality

**Directions**: *To help you understand the differences between dialogue form and narrative form, complete the following activity. For each excerpt in dialogue form, convert it to narrative form. Once you have converted the dialogue, describe the purpose(s) served by each excerpt of dialogue. An example has been done for you. If you need more room for your answers, use a separate sheet of paper.*

***Example:***
*Dialogue Form:*
Lennie looked timidly over to him. "George?"
    "Yeah, what ya want?"
    "Where we goin', George?"
The little man jerked down the brim of his hat and scowled over at Lennie.
    "So you forgot awready, did you? I gotta tell you again, do I? Jesus Christ, you're a crazy bastard!"

*Narrative Form:* Lennie looked over timidly at George. With a strange, confused apprehension he asked where they were headed. Angry and irritated over hearing the same question at least ten times, George snapped and yelled at Lennie.

*Specific Purpose:* By the way George scolds Lennie, we can see that George easily loses his patience with Lennie. There is also evidence of a dialect, although we are not completely clear which dialect it is.

1. *Dialogue Form:*
    "Ain't a thing in my pocket," Lennie said cleverly.
    "I know there ain't. You got it in your hand. What you got in your hand—hidin' it?"
    "I ain't got nothin', George. Honest."
    "Come on, give it here."
Lennie held his closed hand away from George's direction. "It's only a mouse, George."
    "A mouse? A live mouse?"
    "Uh-uh. Jus' a dead mouse, George. I didn' kill it. Honest! I found it. I found it dead."

Name _____ Period _____

*Narrative Form:*

_____
_____
_____

Specific Purpose:

_____
_____
_____

2. *Dialogue Form:*
    "O.K. Now when we go in to see the boss, what you gonna do?"
    "I… I," Lennie thought. His face grew tight with thought. "I … ain't gonna say nothin'. Jus' gonna stan' there."
    "Good boy. That's swell. You say that over two, three times so you won't forget it." Lennie droned to himself softly. "I ain't gonna say nothin'… I ain't gonna say nothin'… I ain't gonna say nothin'."

*Narrative Form:*

_____
_____
_____

Specific Purpose:

_____
_____
_____

3. *Dialogue Form:*
    "George," very softly. No answer. "George!"
    "Whatta you want?"
    "I was only foolin', George. I don't want no ketchup. I wouldn't eat no ketchup if it was right here beside me."
    "If it was here, you could have some."
    "But I wouldn't eat none, George, I'd leave it all for you. You could cover your beans with it and I wouldn't touch none of it."

*Narrative Form:*

_____
_____
_____

Specific Purpose:

_____

Name _____ Period _____

_____
_____

4. *Dialogue Form:*
Lennie spoke craftily, "Tell me—like you done before."
   "Tell you what?"
   "About the rabbits."
George snapped, "You ain't gonna put nothing over on me."
Lennie pleaded, "Come on, George. Tell me. Please, George. Like you done before."
   "You get a kick outta that, don't you? Awright, I'll tell you, and then we'll eat our supper…."

*Narrative Form:*
_____
_____
_____

*Specific Purpose:*
_____
_____

5. Steinbeck uses dialogue with dialect and slang, even using curse words and the word "nigger", to make his characters sound more realistic. How would the novel be different if Steinbeck used Standard English (no dialect, slang, or curse words), rather than this more naturalistic vocabulary? Explain. _____
_____
_____

6. Many schools have banned *Of Mice and Men* because of the use of the word "nigger" and other curse words. What is your reaction to schools banning the book for these reasons? _____
_____
_____

7. Steinbeck once wrote "For too long the language of books was different from the language of men. To the men I write about profanity is adornment and ornament and is never vulgar and I write it so." What do you think Steinbeck means when he says that "profanity is adornment and ornament"? Do you agree? Explain your thoughts.
_____
_____
_____
_____

Name _____ Period _____

# Chapter One
*Assessment Preparation: Word Analysis*

Do you realize that you actually know more words than you think you do? There are common prefixes and suffixes that you use on a daily basis that can help you to figure out words you may have never seen before.

For example, we have all heard or seen the word *swimmer*. This word breaks down into the base word *swim*, plus the suffix *–er*. The suffixes *–er* or *–or* mean *someone or something that undergoes an action*. Therefore, the word *swimmer* means "someone or something that swims." Similarly, the word *baker* means "someone or something that bakes." Can you guess what the word *motivator* means?

Adding a prefix or a suffix can also change the part of speech or the tense of a word. For example, the word *invite* is a verb. If we add the suffix *–tion* to the word, the suffix changes the word from the verb *invite* to the word *invit(a)tion*, which is a noun. The tense of a verb changes from present tense to past tense when *–ed* is added, for example, *ignore* to *ignored*. There are many prefixes and suffixes that you use regularly that can help you figure out the vocabulary words from the novel.

***Directions:*** *Use a dictionary to help you analyze the vocabulary words from Chapter One. Be sure to note whether the word is already in its base form (no prefixes or suffixes have been added), or whether a prefix or suffix has been added. On line a., indicate the part of speech of the word, then write down the* <u>base</u> *word's definition. If there is more than one definition, write down the first two. On line b., write the definition of the vocabulary word. On line c., once you have analyzed the word, find the sentence in which the word is used in your text and write it. Finally on line d., using what you have learned about the word, write an original sentence in which you correctly use the vocabulary word. An example has been done for you.*

**Ex.** **morosely**   base: <u> morose </u>   prefix: <u> none </u>   suffix: <u> -ly </u>
   a. Part of Speech (POS), definition of base: <u>adj.; having a withdrawn or gloomy personality</u>
   b. POS, definition of vocabulary word: <u>adv.; in a withdrawn or gloomy manner</u>
   c. Sentence from text: <u>George stared morosely at the water.</u>
   d. Original sentence: <u>The children walked morosely to school on the first day back from summer vacation.</u>

1. **junctures**   base: _____   prefix: _____   suffix: _____
   a. POS, definition of base: _____
   _____
   b. POS, definition of vocabulary word: _____
   _____

**Name** _____   **Period** _____

   c. Sentence from text: _____

_____

_____

   d. Original sentence: _____

_____

_____

2. **debris**   base: _____   prefix: _____   suffix: _____

   a. POS, definition of base: _____

_____

   b. POS, definition of vocabulary word: _____

_____

   c. Sentence from text: _____

_____

_____

   d. Original sentence: _____

_____

_____

3. **mottled**   base: _____   prefix: _____   suffix: _____

   a. POS, definition of base: _____

_____

   b. POS, definition of vocabulary word: _____

_____

   c. Sentence from text: _____

_____

_____

   d. Original sentence: _____

_____

_____

4. **recumbent**   base: _____   prefix: _____   suffix: _____

   a. POS, definition of base: _____

_____

   b. POS, definition of vocabulary word: _____

_____

**Name** _____   **Period** _____

   c. Sentence from text: _____

_____

   d. Original sentence: _____

_____

5. **lumbered**   base: _____ prefix: _____ suffix: _____

   a. POS, definition of base: _____

_____

   b. POS, definition of vocabulary word: _____

_____

   c. Sentence from text: _____

_____

   d. Original sentence: _____

_____

6. **brusquely**   base: _____ prefix: _____ suffix: _____

   a. POS, definition of base: _____

_____

   b. POS, definition of vocabulary word: _____

_____

   c. Sentence from text: _____

_____

   d. Original sentence: _____

_____

7. **pantomime**   base: _____ prefix: _____ suffix: _____

   a. POS, definition of base: _____

_____

   b. POS, definition of vocabulary word: _____

_____

**Name** _____   **Period** _____

   c. Sentence from text: _____
_____
_____

   d. Original sentence: _____
_____
_____

8. **contemplated**  base: _____  prefix: _____  suffix: _____

   a. POS, definition of base: _____
_____

   b. POS, definition of vocabulary word: _____
_____

   c. Sentence from text: _____
_____
_____

   d. Original sentence: _____
_____
_____

9. **imperiously**  base: _____  prefix: _____  suffix: _____

   a. POS, definition of base: _____
_____

   b. POS, definition of vocabulary word: _____
_____

   c. Sentence from text: _____
_____
_____

   d. Original sentence: _____
_____
_____

10. **anguished**  base: _____  prefix: _____  suffix: _____

   a. POS, definition of base: _____
_____

   b. POS, definition of vocabulary word: _____
_____

**Name** _____  **Period** _____

   c. Sentence from text: _____

_____

   d. Original sentence: _____

_____

_____

11. **yammered**   base: _____  prefix: _____  suffix: _____

   a. POS, definition of base: _____

_____

   b. POS, definition of vocabulary word: _____

_____

   c. Sentence from text: _____

_____

_____

   d. Original sentence: _____

_____

_____

Name _____  Period _____

# Chapter Two
*Note-Taking and Summarizing*

| | |
|---|---|
| **Question** | |
| **Connect** | |
| **Comprehension Check Notes** | |
| **Summarize** | |
| **Predict** | |
| **Reflect** | |

Name _____    Period _____

# Chapter Two
*Comprehension Check*

**Directions**: *To give you a comprehensive understanding of all aspects of the novel, answer the following questions using complete sentences on a separate sheet of paper. Be sure to use your Note-Taking chart to keep important notes for each chapter and to help you answer the Comprehension Check questions.*

1. What does George find in the box by his bed and what does he assume? What does this tell you about the living conditions of the migrant workers?
2. Why is the boss suspicious of George? How does George explain his relationship with Lennie? Why do you think George lies?
3. Describe Curley. What does the swamper tell George about Curley's left hand?
4. Describe Curley's wife, according to the swamper.
5. Why does George warn Lennie to stay away from Curley? What does George tell Lennie to do if there is trouble?
6. Why does Lennie suddenly want to leave the ranch?
7. What does Carlson suggest about Candy's old dog? How do you feel about Carlson's suggestion?
8. Use the description at the beginning of Chapter Two to draw a detailed picture of the bunkhouse.

**Name** _____   **Period** _____

## Chapter Two
*Standards Focus: Analyzing Poetry*

While some students may think that the title *Of Mice and Men* comes from the fact that Lennie likes to pet mice and other soft things, the title is really taken from the poem "To a Mouse" by Robert Burns. Robert Burns (*1759 - 1796*) is probably the most famous of all the Scottish poets. After accidentally turning up a mouse's nest while he was plowing in 1785, he wrote an ode to this mouse, expressing his feelings toward the mouse and his home.

For the average English speaker, Burns's poetry can be quite archaic and complex. On the left is the original poem by Burns. On the right is a translation of the words into modern English.

| | |
|---|---|
| Wee, sleekit, cowran, tim'rous beastie, | Small, sleek, cowardly, nervous little beast, |
| O, what panic's in thy breastie! | Oh, what a panic is in your breast! |
| Thou need na start awa sae hasty, | You need not run away so hastily, |
| Wi' bickering brattle! | With a quick scurry! |
| I wad be laith to rin an' chase thee, | I would hate to run and chase you, |
| Wi' murd'ring pattle! | With a murdering shovel! |
| | |
| I'm truly sorry Man's dominion | I am truly sorry that Man's power |
| Has broken Nature's social union, | Has broken Nature's union between man and beast |
| An' justifies that ill opinion, | And justifies that sad opinion |
| Which makes thee startle, | Which makes you startle, |
| At me, thy poor, earth-born companion, | At me, your poor, earth-born friend, |
| An' fellow-mortal! | And fellow mortal! |
| | |
| I doubt na, whyles, but thou may thieve; | I do not doubt that sometimes you may steal; |
| What then? poor beastie, thou maun live! | But so what? Poor beast, you must also live! |
| A daimen-icker in a thrave 's a sma' request: | A corn stalk in a field is a small request: |
| I'll get a blessin wi' the lave, | I will be blessed with more, |
| An' never miss't! | And will never miss it! |
| | |
| Thy wee-bit housie, too, in ruin! | Your tiny little house, now, is ruined! |
| It's silly wa's the win's are strewin! | Its impractical walls the winds are blowing! |
| An' naething, now, to big a new ane, | And nothing now, to build a new one, |
| O' foggage green! | Of green foliage! |
| An' bleak December's winds ensuin, | And bleak December's wind beginning, |
| Baith snell an' keen! | Both severe and sharp! |
| | |
| Thou saw the fields laid bare an' wast, | You saw the fields bare and vast, |
| An' weary Winter comin fast, | And the tired Winter coming fast, |
| An' cozie here, beneath the blast, | And cozy here, beneath the hearth, |
| Thou thought to dwell, | You thought to make your home, |
| Till crash! the cruel coulter past | Until crash! the cruel plow passed |
| Out thro' thy cell. | And destroyed your home. |
| | |
| That wee-bit heap o' leaves an' stibble, | That tiny, little heap of leaves and sticks, |
| Has cost thee monie a weary nibble! | Has cost you many a tired nibble! |
| Now thou's turn'd out, for a' thy trouble, | Now you are homeless for all of your trouble, |
| But house or hald. | Without house or home. |
| To thole the Winter's sleety dribble, | To live in the Winter's sleety dribble, |
| An' cranreuch cauld! | And harsh cold! |

©2009 Secondary Solutions          *Of Mice and Men* Literature Guide

**Name** _____  **Period** _____

## Standards Focus: Analyzing Poetry

| | |
|---|---|
| But Mousie, thou are no thy-lane, | But Mousie, you are not alone, |
| In proving foresight may be vain: | Your planning may be in vain: |
| **The best laid schemes o' Mice an' Men,** | **The best laid plans of Mice and of Men,** |
| **Gang aft agley,** | **Often go awry,** |
| An' lea'e us nought but grief an' pain, | And leave us nothing but grief and pain, |
| For promis'd joy! | For the joy we expected! |
| | |
| Still, thou art blest, compar'd wi' me! | Still, you are blessed, compared with me! |
| The present only toucheth thee: | The present moment only affects you: |
| But Och! I backward cast my e'e, | But Oh! I think back |
| On prospects drear! | On sad moments! |
| An' forward, tho' I canna see, | And although I cannot see my life ahead |
| I guess an' fear! | I guess what may be, and I am afraid! |

**Directions**: After reading the original poem and the translation, answer the following questions on a separate piece of paper.

1. _____ The author's attitude toward the mouse is best described as:
    a. sympathetic    c. heartless
    b. skeptical      d. aloof

2. Use a dictionary to look up the word "awry." What do you think Burns meant by "*The best laid plans of Mice and of Men / Often go awry*"?

3. Which statement best describes the theme of this poem?
    a. Men are superior to mice and other small creatures.
    b. Life is made up of the simpler moments.
    c. Nature may not always be around, so we should appreciate it while we can.
    d. Even the most well-constructed plans can fail.

4. Why do you think Steinbeck chose his title from this poem?

5. What kind of ending do you think the novel will have, based upon what you have learned from the theme of this poem?

6. Many of us look back on our lives and although we may have had the best intentions or plans, things did not work out the way we wanted them to, for one reason or another. Think about a time that you had planned for something to turn out one way, and it ended up another. What was the situation? What was your reaction? How did you adapt to the situation? How are you dealing with the situation now? Would you have done anything differently, knowing what you know now?

**Bonus:** Write a short poem expressing what happens when you have a dream and it doesn't come true.

Name _____    Period _____

# Chapter Two
*Assessment Preparation: Context Clues*

In most assessments, you must infer (make an educated guess) the meanings of words by looking at **context clues**, or clues within an entire sentence. You must look at *how* the word is used in the sentence in order to make an inference.

***Directions***: *For each vocabulary word from Chapter Two, first indicate the part of speech in which the vocabulary word appears (noun, verb, etc.). Then write an original definition for the vocabulary word **based upon the clues in the sentence**. (If you need further clarification, read the entire paragraph on the page number given in parentheses.) Finally, look up the word and write down the dictionary definition. How accurate is your definition?*

**Ex.** And these shelves were loaded with little articles, soap and talcum powder, razors and those Western magazines ranch men love to read and <u>scoff</u> at and secretly believe.

   a. Part of Speech: <u>verb</u>

   b. Inference: <u>laugh at; make fun of</u>

   c. Definition: <u>to express ridicule or contempt towards or about somebody or something</u>

1. "A guy on a ranch don't never listen nor he don't ask no questions."
   "Damn right he don't," said George, slightly <u>mollified</u>, "not if he wants to stay workin' long." (25)

   a. Part of Speech: _____
   b. Inference: _____
   c. Definition: _____

2. His glance was at once calculating and <u>pugnacious</u>. Lennie squirmed under the look and shifted his feet nervously. (25)

   a. Part of Speech: _____
   b. Inference: _____
   c. Definition: _____

3. Curley stepped <u>gingerly</u> close to him. "You the new guys the old man was waitin' for?" (25)

   a. Part of Speech: _____
   b. Inference: _____
   c. Definition: _____

4. "Curley's pretty <u>handy</u>. He's done quite a bit in the ring. He's a lightweight, and he's handy." (26)

   a. Part of Speech: _____
   b. Inference: _____

**Name** _____   **Period** _____

    c. Definition: _____

5. George was watching the door. He said <u>ominously</u>, "Well, he better watch out for Lennie." (27)

    a. Part of Speech: _____

    b. Inference: _____

    c. Definition: _____

6. "Don't tell Curley I said none of this. He'd <u>slough</u> me. He just don't give a damn." (27)

    a. Part of Speech: _____

    b. Inference: _____

    c. Definition: _____

7. "That's a dirty thing to tell around," he (George) said. The old man was reassured. He had drawn a <u>derogatory</u> statement from George. (28)

    a. Part of Speech: _____

    b. Inference: _____

    c. Definition: _____

8. George stared at his solitaire lay, and then he <u>flounced</u> the cards together and turned around to Lennie. (29)

    a. Part of Speech: _____

    b. Inference: _____

    c. Definition: _____

9. Lennie's eyes were frightened. "I don't want no trouble," he said <u>plaintively</u>. "Don't let him sock me, George." (29)

    a. Part of Speech: _____

    b. Inference: _____

    c. Definition: _____

10. His tone grew <u>decisive</u>. "You keep away from Curley, Lennie." (30)

    a. Part of Speech: _____

    b. Inference: _____

    c. Definition: _____

11. Lennie, who had been following the conversation back and forth with his eyes, smiled <u>complacently</u> at the compliment. (34)

    a. Part of Speech: _____

    b. Inference: _____

    c. Definition: _____

Name _____  Period _____

## Chapter Three
*Note-Taking and Summarizing*

| | |
|---|---|
| **Question** | |
| **Connect** | |
| **Comprehension Check Notes** | |
| **Summarize** | |
| **Predict** | |
| **Reflect** | |

Name _____  Period _____

# Chapter Three
*Comprehension Check*

**Directions**: *To give you a comprehensive understanding of all aspects of the novel, answer the following questions using complete sentences on a separate sheet of paper. Be sure to use your Note-Taking chart to keep important notes for each chapter and to help you answer the Comprehension Check questions.*

1. What does Slim find "funny" about George and Lennie's relationship? How does George explain his relationship with Lennie?
2. Why did George stop teasing Lennie? What does this tell you about George's character?
3. Why do you think the girl in Weed claimed that Lennie tried to rape her?
4. Why do you think George tells Slim the story of what happened to them in Weed?
5. Why doesn't George want Lennie to sleep with the puppy in his bed?
6. How do the men like to spend their money and free time on the weekends?
7. Describe the offer Candy makes to George. What is George's first reaction? What does he then decide? What changes his mind?
8. How did Candy get $250?
9. Why is Lennie smiling when Curley comes in?
10. Why does Candy regret not shooting his dog himself?
11. What happens as a result of Curley's attack on Lennie?
12. What does Slim make Curley agree to? Why does he make Curley do this? What does this tell you about Slim's character?
13. How is Candy like his dog? Why is the shooting of Candy's dog so difficult on Candy?

Name _____   Period _____

# Chapter Three
*Standards Focus: Recognizing Vivid Details*

**Directions**: *Read the following excerpts from Chapter Three, <u>underlining</u> each word that evokes some sensory stimulation (sight, sound, smell, touch, taste). Then answer the questions that follow.*

Excerpt #1
　　They took places opposite each other at the table under the light, but George did not shuffle the cards. He rippled the edge of the deck nervously, and the little snapping noise drew the eyes of all the men in the room, so that he stopped doing it. The silence fell on the room again. A minute passed, and another minute. Candy lay still, staring at the ceiling. Slim gazed at him for a moment and then looked down at his hands; he subdued one hand with the other, and held it down. There came a little gnawing sound from under the floor and all the men looked down toward it gratefully. Only Candy continued to stare at the ceiling.

1. _____ To what senses is Steinbeck appealing in this paragraph?
    a. smell and touch           c. touch and sound
    b. smell and sight           d. sight and sound

2. _____ How is the information in this paragraph organized?
    a. order of importance (most to least *or* least to most important)
    b. chronological order (the order in which the events occurred)
    c. spatial order (description of the space or surroundings)
    d. order of sensory description (description of what you see, hear, taste, etc.)

3. _____ What mood pervades most of the paragraph?
    a. delight           c. anxiety
    b. embarrassment     d. loneliness

4. _____ Which of the following can you infer from the information given in the paragraph?
    a. The men want to play cards.
    b. The men do not know what to say or do.
    c. Candy was not invited to play cards
    d. Slim wants to console Candy.

5. Why do you think Steinbeck included this paragraph in the novel? _____
_____
_____

Excerpt #2
　　George's hands stopped working with the cards. His voice was growing warmer. "An' we could have a few pigs. I could build a smoke house like the one gran'pa had, an' when we kill a pig we can smoke the bacon and the hams, and make sausage an' all like that. An' when the salmon run up river we could catch a hundred of 'em an' salt 'em down or smoke 'em. We could have them for breakfast. They ain't nothing so nice as smoked salmon. When the fruit come in we could can it—and tomatoes, they're easy to can. Ever' Sunday we'd kill a chicken or a rabbit. Maybe we'd have a cow or a goat, and the cream is so God damn thick you got to cut it with a knife and take it out with a spoon."

Name _____    Period _____

*Lennie watched him with wide eyes, and old Candy watched him too. Lennie said softly, "We could live offa the fatta the lan'."*

6. _____ What senses are used to define the setting in this excerpt?
   a. smell and touch
   b. sight and sound
   c. taste and sound
   d. sight and taste

7. _____ How would you describe the mood of the passage?
   a. sullen
   b. optimistic
   c. festive
   d. tense

8. How does this paragraph reflect the time period in which it was written? In other words, what things are mentioned that may not be found or used in our society today? Explain. _____
   _____
   _____
   _____

Excerpt #3

*Then Curley's rage exploded. "Come on, ya big bastard. Get up on your feet. No big son-of-a-bitch is gonna laugh at me. I'll show ya who's yella."*

*Lennie looked helplessly at George, and then he got up and tried to retreat. Curley was balanced and poised. He dashed at Lennie with his left, and then smashed down his nose with a right. Lennie gave a cry of terror. Blood welled from his nose. "George," he cried. "Make 'um let me alone, George." He backed until he was against the wall, and Curley followed, slugging him in the face. Lennie's hands remained at his sides; he was too frightened to defend himself.*

*George was on his feet yelling. "Get him, Lennie. Don't let him do it."*

*Lennie covered his face with his huge paws and bleated with terror. He cried, "Make 'um stop, George." Then Curley attacked his stomach and cut off his wind.*

9. _____ To what senses is Steinbeck appealing in this excerpt?
   a. smell and touch
   b. smell and sight
   c. touch and sound
   d. sight and sound

10. _____ What mood pervades most of the paragraph?
    a. anxiety
    b. frustration
    c. tension
    d. humiliation

11. Steinbeck uses mostly short, choppy sentences in these few paragraphs in order to enhance the effect of the scene. Explain how sentence length helps to contribute to the mood of the scene. _____
    _____
    _____
    _____

**Name** _____  **Period** _____

# Chapter Three
*Assessment Preparation:* Word Origins

**Directions**: For each of the vocabulary words from Chapter Three below:
   a. Read the origin of the word.
   b. Draw an inference of the vocabulary word's meaning based upon the word origin.
   c. Look up the meaning in a dictionary.
   d. Use the correct definition in a complete sentence, showing that you understand what the vocabulary word means.

**Ex. reprehensible**
   a. Word Origin: from Latin *reprehéns*, meaning "to reprehend" + *ibilis* (ible)
   b. My Definition: able to reprehend; to criticize
   c. Dictionary Definition: deserving criticism; highly unnacceptable
   d. Sentence: Mark's behavior in school was reprehensible—he was always getting in trouble for one thing or another.

1. **derision**
   a. Word Origin: (deride) from Middle English *derisioun* equiv. to L *derīs(us)*, meaning "mocked" (of *derīdére;* deride + ion)
   b. My Definition: _____
   c. Dictionary Definition: _____
   _____
   d. Sentence: _____
   _____

2. **lynch**
   a. Word Origin: *Americanism*; from *lynch-laws,* after the hearings presided over by William *Lynch* (1742–1820)
   b. My Definition: _____
   c. Dictionary Definition: _____
   _____
   d. Sentence: _____
   _____

3. **concealing**
   a. Word Origin: (conceal) from Latin *concélāre,* equiv. to *con-* + *célāre*, meaning "to hide"
   b. My Definition: _____
   c. Dictionary Definition: _____
   _____

**Name** _____  **Period** _____

    d. Sentence: _____
_____

4. **stride**
    a. Word Origin: from Old English *stridan*, meaning "to straddle," from base *strid-* meaning "to strive; make a strong effort"
    b. My Definition: _____
    c. Dictionary Definition: _____
    _____
    d. Sentence: _____
    _____

5. **gnawing**
    a. Word Origin: from Old English *gnagan*, probably imitative of the action of gnawing
    b. My Definition: _____
    c. Dictionary Definition: _____
    _____
    d. Sentence: _____
    _____

6. **entranced**
    a. Word Origin: (entrance) from *en-*, meaning "put in," plus Latin *transire* meaning "cross over (often into death)"
    b. My Definition: _____
    c. Dictionary Definition: _____
    _____
    d. Sentence: _____
    _____

7. **bemused**
    a. Word Origin: (bemuse) from *be-*, meaning "to be," plus Middle English *musen*, meaning "to gaze meditatively on; to be astonished"
    b. My Definition: _____
    c. Dictionary Definition: _____
    _____
    d. Sentence: _____
    _____

**Name** _____ **Period** _____

8. **cowering**
   a. Word Origin: <u>(cower) from Middle English *couren*, meaning "lie in wait"</u>
   b. My Definition: _____
   c. Dictionary Definition: _____
   _____
   d. Sentence: _____
   _____

9. **regarded**
   a. Word Origin: <u>(regard) from Old French *regard*, from *regarder*, meaning "take notice of," from *re-* + *guarder*, meaning "to guard"</u>
   b. My Definition: _____
   c. Dictionary Definition: _____
   _____
   d. Sentence: _____
   _____

10. **wryly**
    a. Word Origin: <u>(wry) from Old English *wrigian*, meaning "to turn; bend; move; go"</u>
    b. My Definition: _____
    c. Dictionary Definition: _____
    _____
    d. Sentence: _____
    _____

11. **solemnly**
    a. Word Origin: <u>(solemn) from Latin *sōlemnis*, meaning "consecrated, holy"</u>
    b. My Definition: _____
    c. Dictionary Definition: _____
    _____
    d. Sentence: _____
    _____

Name _____ Period _____

# Chapter Four
*Note-Taking and Summarizing*

| | |
|---|---|
| **Question** | |
| **Connect** | |
| **Comprehension Check Notes** | |
| **Summarize** | |
| **Predict** | |
| **Reflect** | |

Name _____   Period _____

# Chapter Four
*Comprehension Check*

**Directions**: *To give you a comprehensive understanding of all aspects of the novel, answer the following questions using complete sentences on a separate sheet of paper. Be sure to use your Note-Taking chart to keep important notes for each chapter and to help you answer the Comprehension Check questions.*

1. How is Crooks's living quarters different from the men's bunk houses?
2. For what reason does Lennie go to the barn?
3. How does Crooks react to Lennie when he comes to visit? Why does he react this way?
4. What do we learn about Crooks's family life?
5. Crooks teases Lennie about George leaving him. Why do you think Crooks does this?
6. How does Crooks truly feel about Lennie and Candy's visit?
7. Why does Crooks doubt George and Lennie and Candy's goal of acquiring land?
8. What does Curley's wife say she could have done instead of marrying Curley?
9. How does Curley's wife threaten Crooks?
10. Why does Crooks say he was "jes foolin'" about working at the ranch? Do you believe he really didn't mean it? Why do you think he changes his mind?

Name _____  Period _____

# Chapter Four
*Standards Focus: Conflict and Effect*

One of the most important elements of any type of literature is the development of conflict. **Conflict** is when a character or characters face a struggle or challenge. Without conflict, the reader or audience says, "Who cares?" Just as in our lives we face conflict, so do the characters in great literature. There are four main types of conflict that a character or characters may face within a work of literature:

- **man versus man**—a character faces a conflict/struggle with another character in the story
- **man versus himself**—a character faces a major decision or a physical or emotional struggle with his own morals, ethics, or conscience
- **man versus nature**—a character faces the forces of nature, such as weather or natural environment
- **man versus society**—a character faces a conflict with the social, political, or religious forces of society

In *Of Mice and Men*, conflict surrounds the plot and is a major part of the action. Several conflicts emerge at the same time, and ultimately cause the plot to materialize into an interesting and suspenseful story.

**Directions**: For each situation from Chapters 1-4 below, identify the type of conflict the situation represents and then identify the effect that the conflict has had on the plot so far. An example has been done for you.

| Conflict | Type of Conflict | Effect |
|---|---|---|
| George gets frustrated and irritated with the fact that Lennie has trouble remembering things, and often scolds him for forgetting. | man versus man | George has to take care of Lennie as if he were a child, like carrying his work card for him, and speaking on his behalf. |
| 1) Lennie likes to pet soft things, such as mice, but tends to pet them too hard and kill them, unaware of his own strength. | | |
| 2) George complains that if he didn't have to take care of Lennie he would have a better life, and would be able to do the things he always wanted to do. | | |

Name _____  Period _____

| Conflict | Type of Conflict | Effect |
|---|---|---|
| 3) George and Lennie dream of one day being able to own their own farm, and to work only for themselves, but for now they must work to survive. | | |
| 4) Curley, who has been known to pick fights with bigger men, picks a fight with Lennie. | | |
| 5) Curley is jealous and suspicious of his wife, who seems to flaunt herself in front of other men. | | |
| 6) Crooks lives apart from the other men, ostracized, merely because he is African-American. | | |

**Name** _____   **Period** _____

# Chapter Four
*Assessment Preparation: Word Roots*

**Directions**: Use the word list below from Chapter Four to answer the following. On line a., choose the vocabulary word that has the same root as the hint word given in bold lettering. On line b., give the part of speech and definition of the vocabulary word. Finally, on line c., explain how the hint word and the vocabulary word are connected. An example has been done for you.

| mauled | aloof | meager | liniment | fawning | disarming |
|--------|-------|--------|----------|---------|-----------|
| scornful | brutally | indignation | averted | appraised | crestfallen |

**Ex.** The word **mallet** comes from the L. *malleus,* meaning "hammer," from *mele-,* meaning "to grind, crush"

    a. Which vocabulary word has this same root? _____ mauled _____

    b. Definition of vocabulary word: <u>verb; to handle or use roughly</u>

    c. How the words are connected: <u>The word mallet and the word mauled both have to do with handling roughly; a mallet can be used to maul something</u>

1. The word **crest** is from the Latin *crista* meaning "tuft; plume," perhaps related to the word for "hair."

    a. Which vocabulary word has this same root? _____

    b. Definition of vocabulary word: _____

    c. How the words are connected: _____

2. The word **emaciate** comes from the Latin *emaciare,* meaning "to waste away," from *ex-,* meaning "out" + *macer,* meaning "thin"

    a. Which vocabulary word has this same root? _____

    b. Definition of vocabulary word: _____

    c. How the words are connected: _____

3. The word **versus** comes from the Latin *versus,* meaning "turned toward or against"

    a. Which vocabulary word has this same root? _____

**Name** _____  **Period** _____

    b. Definition of vocabulary word: _____

    _____

    c. How the words are connected: _____

    _____

4. The word **armor** comes from the Old French *arma*, meaning "weapons"

    a. Which vocabulary word has this same root? _____

    b. Definition of vocabulary word: _____

    _____

    c. How the words are connected: _____

    _____

5. The word **brute** comes from the Latin *brutus*, meaning "heavy; dull; stupid"

    a. Which vocabulary word has this same root? _____

    b. Definition of vocabulary word: _____

    _____

    c. How the words are connected: _____

    _____

6. The word **scorn** comes from the Old French *escarn*, meaning "mockery; derision; contempt"

    a. Which vocabulary word has this same root? _____

    b. Definition of vocabulary word: _____

    _____

    c. How the words are connected: _____

    _____

7. The word **lime** comes from the Old English *lim*, meaning "sticky substance"

    a. Which vocabulary word has this same root? _____

    b. Definition of vocabulary word: _____

    _____

    c. How the words are connected: _____

    _____

**Name** _____  **Period** _____

8. The word **luff** comes from the Middle Dutch *loef, meaning* "windward side of a ship"

    a. Which vocabulary word has this same root? _____

    b. Definition of vocabulary word: _____
    _____

    c. How the words are connected: _____
    _____

9. The word **fain** comes from the Old English *faegen,* meaning "happy" or "fair"

    a. Which vocabulary word has this same root? _____

    b. Definition of vocabulary word: _____
    _____

    c. How the words are connected: _____
    _____

10. The word **prize** comes from the Latin *pretium,* meaning "to think over, consider"

    a. Which vocabulary word has this same root? _____

    b. Definition of vocabulary word: _____
    _____

    c. How the words are connected: _____
    _____

11. The word **decent** comes from the Latin *dignus,* meaning "worthy"

    a. Which vocabulary word has this same root? _____

    b. Definition of vocabulary word: _____
    _____

    c. How the words are connected: _____
    _____

Name _____  Period _____

# Chapter Five
*Note-Taking and Summarizing*

| | |
|---|---|
| **Question** | |
| **Connect** | |
| **Comprehension Check Notes** | |
| **Summarize** | |
| **Predict** | |
| **Reflect** | |

Name _____ Period _____

# Chapter Five
*Comprehension Check*

**Directions**: *To give you a comprehensive understanding of all aspects of the novel, answer the following questions using complete sentences on a separate sheet of paper. Be sure to use your Note-Taking chart to keep important notes for each chapter and to help you answer the Comprehension Check questions.*

1. How did Lennie's puppy die?
2. Why is Lennie angry at his puppy?
3. Why is Lennie so reluctant to talk to Curley's wife?
4. Why does Curley's wife continue talking to Lennie, despite Lennie's protests? What reasons does she give for wanting to talk to him?
5. What does Curley's wife give as the reason the men won't bother them in the barn?
6. Why did Curley's wife rush to marry Curley?
7. Why does Lennie become angry with Curley's wife? What happens as a result?
8. How does Lennie know where to go to avoid getting in trouble?
9. Who finds Curley's wife?
10. Why does George tell Candy to wait until he is gone before calling in the other men?
11. What does Candy now realize that makes him particularly angry towards Curley's wife?
12. What does Carlson think has happened to his Luger?
13. What does Curley say he is going to do to Lennie?
14. Why is Candy so upset at the end of this chapter?

Name _____    Period _____

# Chapter Five
*Standards Focus: Characterization and Character Types*

As authors develop the plot and characters for a story, several *character types* emerge:
- ✓ The **protagonist** of a story is the main character who changes throughout the story; the protagonist is directly affected by the events of the plot.
- ✓ The **antagonist** is the main character in opposition to the protagonist; the antagonist usually causes the protagonist's problems. The antagonist can also be a force of nature.

To further define his characters, an author then develops four general types of characters which evolve around the protagonist and antagonist and support the plot development.
- **Round** characters are complicated and interesting to the reader.
- **Flat** characters are simple and under-developed.
- **Dynamic** characters are those that grow or change emotionally or learn a lesson.
- **Static** characters change or grow very little (or not at all) throughout the story.

To help understand these character types, we must study the way that the author has written about each character. There are several ways we learn about a character:
- **Direct characterization** is when the author or narrator tells the reader what a character is like. For example, "Jennifer is a good student."
- **Indirect characterization** is when the author gives information about a character and allows the reader to draw his or her own conclusions about that character. Two of the ways we can learn about a character through **indirect characterization** are:
  - the character's own thoughts, feelings and actions
  - what other characters say or feel, or how they act towards another character

**Directions**: For each of the characters below, complete the chart with <u>direct quotes</u> of both direct and indirect characterization from Chapters 1-5 of the novel, including page numbers for each. Then, for the last two rows, decide how the character should be classified: protagonist, antagonist, or other, round or flat, dynamic or static. An example has been done for you on the chart on the next page.

*NOTE: It is very important that the quotes you choose for each character actually say something about the character him/herself. Before you write down the quote, ask yourself, what do I learn about the character through this quote? If you don't learn something about the character, you haven't chosen a good quote. See the following example for help.*

**Good Quote**: The boss says about George: "Well, I never seen one guy take so much trouble for another guy." (We learn that George takes care of Lennie and has an unusually close relationship with him.)

**Bad Quote**: George says to Lennie: "You never oughta drink water when it ain't running, Lennie." (This quote won't work because it doesn't help us learn anything about George or Lennie. All it really says is that George warned Lennie.)

Name _____   Period _____

| Character | George |
|---|---|
| Direct Characterization | "The first man was small and quick, dark of face, with restless eyes and sharp, strong features." (page 4) |
| Indirect Characterization | The boss says about George: "Well, I never seen one guy take so much trouble for another guy." (page 23) |
| Inference from Indirect Characterization | George looks out for Lennie and takes care of him like he would his own brother. |
| Protagonist, Antagonist, or Other | Protagonist |
| Round or Flat | Round |
| Dynamic or Static | Dynamic |

| | Lennie | Candy |
|---|---|---|
| Direct Characterization | | |
| Indirect Characterization | | |
| Inference from Indirect Characterization | | |
| Protagonist, Antagonist, or Other | | |
| Round or Flat | | |
| Dynamic or Static | | |

Name _____    Period _____

|  | Curley | Slim |
|---|---|---|
| Direct Characterization | | |
| Indirect Characterization | | |
| Inference from Indirect Characterization | | |
| Protagonist, Antagonist, or Other | | |
| Round or Flat | | |
| Dynamic or Static | | |
|  | **Crooks** | **Curley's Wife** |
| Direct Characterization | | |
| Indirect Characterization | | |
| Inference from Indirect Characterization | | |
| Protagonist, Antagonist, or Other | | |
| Round or Flat | | |
| Dynamic or Static | | |

Name _____    Period _____

# Chapter Five
*Assessment Preparation: Determining Parts of Speech*

Determining the part of speech of a word is very important for assessments, but also for determining the definitions and usage in everyday written language. If you can determine the part of speech for a word you have never seen before, you may also be able to distinguish the word's meaning.

Read the following sentence.

> Suzie was a <u>parsimonious</u> person; she never went out without saving enough money first.

In order to determine a new word's meaning,
1) find the subject(s) of the sentence: Suzie
2) find the predicate(s) (verb) of the sentence: was; went
3) determine how the vocabulary word fits into the sentence: since "Suzie" is the subject and "was" and "went" are the verbs, I know that the vocabulary word is more than likely *not* a noun or verb. Since it is next to the word "person" I can assume that the word is describing Suzie. Additionally, I know that the suffix "–ous" means "full of," and it changes a noun to an adjective, so I am able to determine that the word is an *adjective*.
4) From here, I can use the other context clues in the sentence to find the correct definition. *Note: you may not always have context information to guess a word's meaning. When that is the case, you may want to read a few sentences before and after the vocabulary word in order to see if you can infer the word's meaning. (For this exercise, page numbers have been given to help you. If you still need help, refer to a dictionary.)*

**Directions**: Read each sentence from Chapter Five, Determine the part of speech in context for each underlined vocabulary word as you complete the chart. An example has been done for you.

| Word in Context | "From outside came the clang of horseshoes on the playing [1] peg and the shouts of men, playing [2], encouraging, <u>jeering</u>." (pg. 82) | | |
|---|---|---|---|
| Subject(s) | Predicate(s) | Part of Speech of Vocabulary Word | Definition of Vocabulary Word |
| men | came | verb | laughing at or mocking scornfully |

(In this example, playing [2], encouraging, and jeering are all "participles", not verbs)

| Word in Context | (1) "He picked up the pup and <u>hurled</u> it from him." (pg. 83) | | |
|---|---|---|---|
| Subject(s) | Predicate(s) | Part of Speech of Vocabulary Word | Definition of Vocabulary Word |
|  |  |  |  |

Name _____ Period _____

| Word in Context | (2) | "He looked <u>sullenly</u> up at her." (pg. 84) | |
|---|---|---|---|
| Subject(s) | Predicate(s) | Part of Speech of Vocabulary Word | Definition of Vocabulary Word |
| | | | |

| Word in Context | (3) | "Then all of Lennie's <u>woe</u> came back on him." (pg. 84) | |
|---|---|---|---|
| Subject(s) | Predicate(s) | Part of Speech of Vocabulary Word | Definition of Vocabulary Word |
| | | | |

| Word in Context | (4) | "She <u>consoled</u> him." (pg. 85) | |
|---|---|---|---|
| Subject(s) | Predicate(s) | Part of Speech of Vocabulary Word | Definition of Vocabulary Word |
| | | | |

| Word in Context | (5) | "His face was <u>contorted</u>." (pg. 88) | |
|---|---|---|---|
| Subject(s) | Predicate(s) | Part of Speech of Vocabulary Word | Definition of Vocabulary Word |
| | | | |

| Word in Context | (6) "Her feet battered on the hay and she <u>writhed</u> to be free; and from under Lennie's hand came a muffled screaming." (pg. 88) | | |
|---|---|---|---|
| Subject(s) | Predicate(s) | Part of Speech of Vocabulary Word | Definition of Vocabulary Word |
| | | | |

Name _____    Period _____

| Word in Context | (7) "Her feet battered on the hay and she writhed to be free; and from under Lennie's hand came a <u>muffled</u> screaming." (pg. 88) | | |
|---|---|---|---|
| Subject(s) | Predicate(s) | Part of Speech of Vocabulary Word | Definition of Vocabulary Word |
|  |  |  |  |

| Word in Context | (8) "For a moment he seemed <u>bewildered</u>." (pg. 89) | | |
|---|---|---|---|
| Subject(s) | Predicate(s) | Part of Speech of Vocabulary Word | Definition of Vocabulary Word |
|  |  |  |  |

| Word in Context | (9) "He <u>pawed</u> up the hay until it partly covered her." (pg. 89) | | |
|---|---|---|---|
| Subject(s) | Predicate(s) | Part of Speech of Vocabulary Word | Definition of Vocabulary Word |
|  |  |  |  |

| Word in Context | (10) "She whimpered and <u>cringed</u> to the packing box, and jumped in among the puppies." (pg. 90) | | |
|---|---|---|---|
| Subject(s) | Predicate(s) | Part of Speech of Vocabulary Word | Definition of Vocabulary Word |
|  |  |  |  |

| Word in Context | (11) "He <u>sniveled</u>, and his voice shook." (pg. 93) | | |
|---|---|---|---|
| Subject(s) | Predicate(s) | Part of Speech of Vocabulary Word | Definition of Vocabulary Word |
|  |  |  |  |

Name _____  Period _____

# Chapter Six
*Note-Taking and Summarizing*

| | |
|---|---|
| **Question** | |
| **Connect** | |
| **Comprehension Check Notes** | |
| **Summarize** | |
| **Predict** | |
| **Reflect** | |

Name _____     Period _____

# Chapter Six
*Comprehension Check*

**Directions**: *To give you a comprehensive understanding of all aspects of the novel, answer the following questions using complete sentences on a separate sheet of paper. Be sure to use your Note-Taking chart to keep important notes for each chapter and to help you answer the Comprehension Check questions.*

1. What is the setting at the beginning of the chapter? Why is this setting familiar?
2. Why do you think Lennie visualizes his Aunt Clara at this particular time? What do they "talk" about?
3. What does Lennie "see" next? What does it keep repeating to Lennie?
4. How did George suddenly get a gun? Think back…when did he have a chance to get the gun?
5. What is George's intention in telling Lennie the "story" again at this point?
6. Why do you think George chooses to shoot Lennie? Is this choice fair to Lennie? Why or why not?
7. What might have happened to Lennie if Curley got ahold of him?
8. How does George's version of what happened contradict what actually happened? Why do you think George lies?
9. Some people may feel that Lennie's death was a mercy killing. In other words, George shooting Lennie was to put Lennie out of his misery and help save him from a worse fate. Do you agree with what George did? Do you think it was a mercy killing or murder? Explain your reasoning.
10. Do you think Lennie was expecting George to shoot him? Why or why not? Use evidence from the text to support your response.
11. At the end of the book, Carlson said, "'Now what the hell ya suppose is eatin' them two guys?'" Why is this question important to the themes of the novel? What doesn't Carlson understand?

Name _____   Period _____

# Chapter Six

*Standards Focus: Theme*

**Theme** is the central idea or message in a work of literature. The theme of a piece of literature should not be confused with the subject of the work, but rather, theme is a general statement about life or human nature. Most themes are not completely obvious and must be inferred by the reader. A reader must take a good look at the entire novel: the title, plot, characters, and setting, which all work together to reveal the themes in a piece of literature.

**Part One**
**Directions**: *Think about the title, plot, setting, and characters to answer the following questions. Write your answers using complete sentences below. If you need more room, use a separate piece of paper.*

1. What other novel, movie, short story, or poem does this story remind you of? In what way? _____
_____
_____

2. What other character from a novel, movie, short story, or poem does Lennie remind you of? Why? _____
_____
_____

3. Now that you have read the novel and analyzed the poem "To a Mouse," how do you think this poem relates to the novel? Do you think the title of the novel is appropriate? Why or why not? _____
_____
_____
_____

4. What was your first reaction to George shooting Lennie? Were his actions appropriate? Was it necessary? Site two examples of alternate decisions George could have made.
_____
_____
_____
_____
_____

**Name** _____  **Period** _____

5. From what you have read in this novel, what do you think Steinbeck is trying to say about the nature of human beings? Write one sentence illustrating what you think is the most important message of the novel. _____

_____

_____

_____

_____

**Part Two**
**Directions**: *For each of the following themes from the novel, write down an incident or example from the plot that best illustrates the theme. An example has been done for you.*

1. Theme: *It is important to have friendship and companionship to get through life.*
   Incident or Example: George and Lennie have a friendship and a bond that is unusual. The men on the farm don't understand it because they don't have that kind of friendship with anyone.

2. Theme: *It is important to have dreams for the future.*
   Incident or Example: _____

_____

_____

3. Theme: *Many people live a life of sadness and loneliness, yearning for a connection with another human being.*
   Incident or Example: _____

_____

_____

4. Theme: *It is important for the strong and able to help those who are weak and helpless.*
   Incident or Example: _____

_____

_____

5. Theme: *The American dream never comes true.*
   Incident or Example: _____

_____

_____

Name _____  Period _____

# Chapter Six
*Assessment Preparation: Determining Parts of Speech*

As you did for the *Assessment Preparation* activity for Chapter Five, complete the following activity for Chapter Six, determining the part of speech for each underlined vocabulary word.

**Directions:** Read each sentence in context for each vocabulary word from Chapter Six, completing the chart.

| Word in Context | (1) "A silent head and beak <u>lanced</u> down and plucked it out by the head, and the beak swallowed the little snake while its tail waved frantically." (pg. 97) | | |
|---|---|---|---|
| Subject(s) | Predicate(s) | Part of Speech of Vocabulary Word | Definition of Vocabulary Word |
|  |  |  |  |
| Word in Context | (2) "The sycamore leaves turned up their silver sides, the brown, dry leaves on the ground <u>scudded</u> a few feet." (pg. 97) | | |
| Subject(s) | Predicate(s) | Part of Speech of Vocabulary Word | Definition of Vocabulary Word |
|  |  |  |  |
| Word in Context | (3) "She stood in front of Lennie and put her hands on her hips, and she frowned <u>disapprovingly</u> at him." (pg. 98) | | |
| Subject(s) | Predicate(s) | Part of Speech of Vocabulary Word | Definition of Vocabulary Word |
|  |  |  |  |
| Word in Context | (4) "It sat on its <u>haunches</u> in front of him, and it waggled its ears and crinkled its nose at him." (pg. 99) | | |
| Subject(s) | Predicate(s) | Part of Speech of Vocabulary Word | Definition of Vocabulary Word |
|  |  |  |  |

Name _____   Period _____

| Word in Context | (5) "Now Lennie retorted belligerently." (pg. 100) | | |
|---|---|---|---|
| Subject(s) | Predicate(s) | Part of Speech of Vocabulary Word | Definition of Vocabulary Word |
|  |  |  |  |

| Word in Context | (6) "Now Lennie retorted belligerently." (pg. 100) | | |
|---|---|---|---|
| Subject(s) | Predicate(s) | Part of Speech of Vocabulary Word | Definition of Vocabulary Word |
|  |  |  |  |

| Word in Context | (7) "He said woodenly, 'If I was alone I could live so easy.'" (pg. 101) | | |
|---|---|---|---|
| Subject(s) | Predicate(s) | Part of Speech of Vocabulary Word | Definition of Vocabulary Word |
|  |  |  |  |

| Word in Context | (8) "His voice was monotonous, had no emphasis." (pg. 101) | | |
|---|---|---|---|
| Subject(s) | Predicate(s) | Part of Speech of Vocabulary Word | Definition of Vocabulary Word |
|  |  |  |  |

| Word in Context | (9) "Lennie said craftly—'Tell me like you done before.'" (pg. 101) | | |
|---|---|---|---|
| Subject(s) | Predicate(s) | Part of Speech of Vocabulary Word | Definition of Vocabulary Word |
|  |  |  |  |

Name _____ Period _____

| Word in Context | (10) | "Lennie cried in <u>triumph</u>." (pg. 102) | |
|---|---|---|---|
| Subject(s) | Predicate(s) | Part of Speech of Vocabulary Word | Definition of Vocabulary Word |
| | | | |

| Word in Context | (11) | "Lennie removed his hat <u>dutifully</u> and laid it on the ground in front of him." (pg. 102) | |
|---|---|---|---|
| Subject(s) | Predicate(s) | Part of Speech of Vocabulary Word | Definition of Vocabulary Word |
| | | | |

| Word in Context | (12) | "Lennie <u>jarred</u>, and then settled slowly forward to the sand, and he lay without quivering." (pg. 104) | |
|---|---|---|---|
| Subject(s) | Predicate(s) | Part of Speech of Vocabulary Word | Definition of Vocabulary Word |
| | | | |

Name _____    Period _____

## *Of Mice and Men*
## Quiz: Chapter One

**Directions**: *Write the letter of the best answer on the line provided.*

1. _____ The novel is set in:
   a. Tennessee        c. Alabama
   b. California       d. Virginia

2. _____ What is the name of the town from where George and Lennie have come?
   a. Salinas          c. Weed
   b. Soledad          d. San Francisco

3. _____ What did Lennie want at dinner time?
   a. sausage          c. beans
   b. bread            d. ketchup

4. _____ How are the two men, George and Lennie, different from other migrant workers?
   a. they have lots of money and have chosen to be migrant workers
   b. they own a ranch together
   c. they are brothers
   d. they have a deep connection and friendship

5. _____ What will be Lennie's job on the ranch of their dreams?
   a. taking care of all the livestock      c. light farmwork and general repairs
   b. tending the rabbits                   d. cooking the mens' meals

**Directions**: *Answer each question below using complete sentences.*

6. Explain the relationship between George and Lennie. Who is in charge? Why? What is Lennie's disability? _____

_____

_____

_____

7. What did George want Lennie to do when they got to their new job? _____

_____

8. Describe Lennie and George's dream for the future. _____

_____

_____

_____

Name _____     Period _____

# Of Mice and Men
# Vocabulary Quiz: Chapter One

**Directions:** *Match each vocabulary word with the correct definition or synonym. Write the letter of the correct answer on the line provided.*

1. _____ junctures
2. _____ debris
3. _____ mottled
4. _____ recumbent
5. _____ morosely
6. _____ lumbered
7. _____ brusquely
8. _____ pantomime
9. _____ contemplated
10. _____ imperiously
11. _____ anguished
12. _____ yammered

a. abruptly, angrily, or bluntly in manner or speech
b. with extreme anxiety or torment; distressed
c. fragments of something broken into pieces
d. howled or wailed as if in pain; whimpered
e. in a haughty, dictatorial, or overbearing manner
f. in a withdrawn or gloomy way; sadly; thoughtfully
g. lying back; resting or leaning
h. moved clumsily or heavily
i. points of union; connections
j. spotted; marked with different colors
k. thought deeply about
l. an imitation of someone else's mannerisms

Name _____  Period _____

# *Of Mice and Men*
# Quiz: Chapter Two

**Directions**: *Write the letter of the best answer on the line provided.*

1. _____ When the boss first met George and Lennie, the boss was:
    a. proud and confident
    b. irritated and suspicious
    c. frustrated and tired
    d. excited and nervous

2. _____ The bunkhouses in which the men lived could be described as:
    a. sparse and dim
    b. dark and ornamented
    c. open and airy
    d. personal and comfortable

3. _____ The old dog belonged to:
    a. Curley
    b. Carlson
    c. Candy
    d. Crooks

4. _____ Candy said that Curley picked a fight with Lennie because:
    a. Curley knew Lennie before
    b. Lennie flirted with Curley's wife
    c. Curley doesn't like new guys
    d. Curley doesn't like big guys

5. _____ Candy described Curley's wife as:
    a. pretty, but reserved
    b. lonely and flirtatious
    c. pretty and shy
    d. pretty, but happily married

6. _____ What did George tell Lennie to do if he got in trouble?
    a. call the police
    b. fight back
    c. call him and the boss
    d. run to the river

7. _____ At the end of the chapter, George was afraid:
    a. they would get fired
    b. Lennie would talk to Curley's wife
    c. he would get in a fight with Curley
    d. Lennie would tell their secret to the other men

Name _____  Period _____

# Of Mice and Men
## Vocabulary Quiz: Chapter Two

**Directions:** *Match each vocabulary word with the correct definition or synonym. Write the letter of the correct answer on the line provided.*

1. _____ scoff (at)
2. _____ mollified
3. _____ pugnacious
4. _____ gingerly
5. _____ handy
6. _____ ominously
7. _____ slough
8. _____ derogatory
9. _____ flounced
10. _____ plaintively
11. _____ decisive
12. _____ complacently

a. clever and useful
b. critical or disparaging
c. in a threatening way, indicating something bad is going to happen
d. in a sorrowful or melancholy way; mournfully
e. made to feel better; calmed
f. moved in an exaggerated or angry way
g. able to make decisions quickly; firm
h. to cast something off; shed
i. belligerent or aggressive in nature; quarrelsome
j. to make fun of; tease
k. with self-satisfaction; smugly
l. in a careful or cautious manner

Name _____  Period _____

# *Of Mice and Men*
# Quiz: Chapter Three

**Directions**: Decide whether the statement is true or false. If the statement is true, write the word "true" on the line; if false, write the word "false" on the line and **rewrite** the statement to make it true.

1. _____ After Lennie's Aunt Clara died, George took over care of Lennie.
_____
_____

2. _____ George used to play tricks on Lennie, almost killing him one time.
_____
_____

3. _____ Lennie and George ran from Weed because Lennie raped a girl.
_____
_____

4. _____ Slim shot Candy's dog. _____
_____

5. _____ Candy offered money to be a part of George and Lennie's dream of owning a farm. _____
_____

6. _____ Curley attacked Lennie because he thought Lennie was laughing at him. _____
_____

7. _____ Lennie crushed Curley's hand in the fight. _____
_____

8. _____ Slim ordered Curley to tell the boss about the fight, and to admit he started it. _____
_____
_____

Name _____    Period _____

## Of Mice and Men
## Vocabulary Quiz: Chapter Three

**Directions:** *Match each vocabulary word with the correct definition or synonym. Write the letter of the correct response on the line provided.*

1. _____ derision
2. _____ lynch
3. _____ concealing
4. _____ stride
5. _____ gnawing
6. _____ entranced
7. _____ reprehensible
8. _____ bemused
9. _____ cowering
10. _____ regarded
11. _____ wryly
12. _____ solemnly

a. a long step
b. caused somebody to be confused or puzzled
c. cringing or moving backward defensively in fear
d. highly unacceptable; deserving criticism
e. in a humorless or formal manner
f. in a state of fascination or wonder
g. in an amusing and ironic way
h. mocking scorn; ridicule
i. persistent and troubling
j. putting or keeping someone or something out of sight; hiding
k. thought carefully about someone or something; judged
l. to seize and punish someone believed to have committed a crime

Name _____  Period _____

# *Of Mice and Men*
# Quiz: Chapter Four

***Directions:*** *To assess what you read in Chapter Four, complete the following sentences to the best of your knowledge. There may be more than one correct response, so do the best you can complete each sentence with the word or words that make sense.*

1. While the rest of the men went to town, _____, _____, _____, and _____ were left behind.

2. Crooks could be described as _____ and _____.

3. Crooks was not allowed to play cards with the other men because _____.

4. Crooks told Lennie that if George didn't come back, Lennie would be sent _____.

5. Crooks told Lennie that every man he has met has had the same dream of _____.

6. After hearing Candy and Lennie talk about the plan to buy a farm, _____ also wanted to be a part the plan.

7. Curley's wife told the men that if she had not married Curley, she could have been _____.

8. After George and Lennie left, Crooks told Candy that he _____.

Name _____  Period _____

## Of Mice and Men
## Vocabulary Quiz: Chapter Four

**Directions:** *Match each vocabulary word with the correct definition or synonym. Write the letter of the correct response on the line provided.*

1. _____ mauled
2. _____ aloof
3. _____ meager
4. _____ liniment
5. _____ fawning
6. _____ disarming
7. _____ scornful
8. _____ brutally
9. _____ indignation
10. _____ averted
11. _____ appraised
12. _____ crestfallen

a. downcast, disappointed, or humiliated
b. a pain-relieving cream or ointment
c. anger about an unfairness or wrongdoing
d. attempting to please with flattery
e. charming; friendly or trusting
f. feeling or expressing great contempt for someone or something
g. in an unrelentingly harsh or cruel way
h. looked over; made a judgment about
i. turned away
j. uninvolved with people or events; remote
k. unsatisfactorily small; unsatisfying
l. beat, battered, or tore at a person or animal

Name _____  Period _____

## Of Mice and Men
## Quiz: Chapters Five and Six

***Directions***: *Match the character with the correct description, action, or quote from Chapters Five and Six. Write the letter of the correct answer on the line provided.*

1. _____ Lennie

2. _____ George

3. _____ Candy

4. _____ Slim

5. _____ Carlson

6. _____ Curley

7. _____ Curley's wife

8. _____ Crooks

a. "Why can't I talk to you? I never get to talk to nobody. I get awful lonely."

b. "You done it, di'n't you? I s'pose you're glad. Ever'body knowed you'd mess things up."

c. thought Lennie stole his Luger

d. "I'm gonna shoot the guts outta that big bastard myself, even if I only got one hand."

e. saw a gigantic rabbit

f. "I ain't mad. I never been mad, an' I ain't now. That's a thing I want ya to know."

g. "You hadda, George. I swear you hadda."

h. "I seen it over and over—a guy talkin' to another guy and it don't make no difference if he don't hear or understand."

Name _____     Period _____

## Of Mice and Men
## Vocabulary Quiz: Chapters Five and Six

**Directions:** Match each vocabulary word with the correct definition or synonym. Write the letter of the correct response on the line provided.

1. _____ jeering
2. _____ hurled
3. _____ sullenly
4. _____ woe
5. _____ consoled
6. _____ contorted
7. _____ writhed
8. _____ muffled
9. _____ bewildered
10. _____ pawed
11. _____ cringed
12. _____ sniveled

a. behaved in a whining or self-pitying way
b. in a hostile, unsociable, or morose way
c. completely confused or puzzled
d. greatly bent out of shape
e. grief or distress resulting from serious misfortune
f. provided comfort to someone who is distressed or saddened
g. pulled away in a frightened manner
h. shouting or laughing at someone or something in a mocking or hurtful way
i. struck at repeatedly; touched clumsily
j. threw something with great force
k. twisted or squirmed, especially from feelings of pain
l. padded with material in order to stifle sound

---

13. _____ lanced
14. _____ scudded
15. _____ disapprovingly
16. _____ haunches
17. _____ retorted
18. _____ belligerently
19. _____ woodenly
20. _____ monotonous
21. _____ craftily
22. _____ triumph
23. _____ dutifully
24. _____ jarred

a. an act or occasion of winning or being victorious
b. with negative judgment based upon personal standards
c. hip, buttocks, or upper thigh of an animal
d. in a clever or tricky way
e. in a hostile, aggressive, or fighting manner
f. in an emotionless, unresponsive manner
g. in an obedient manner; without protest
h. moved swiftly and smoothly
i. pierced with a sharp instrument
j. responded in a witty, angry, or insulting manner
k. shook something abruptly
l. uninteresting or boring

Name _____   Period _____

# Of Mice and Men
## Vocabulary Review: Chapters 1-3

**ACROSS**
- 2  to cast something off; shed
- 4  howled or wailed as if in pain; whimpered
- 7  mocking scorn; ridicule
- 10  spotted; marked with different colors
- 11  caused somebody to be confused or puzzled
- 14  in a withdrawn or gloomy way; sadly; thoughtfully
- 15  with self-satisfaction; smugly
- 17  in a state of fascination or wonder
- 20  very carefully
- 24  to make fun of; tease
- 25  highly unacceptable; deserving criticism
- 29  putting or keeping someone or something out of sight; hiding
- 30  a long step
- 31  persistent and troubling
- 32  lying back; resting or leaning
- 33  in a haughty, dictatorial, or overbearing manner
- 34  an imitation of someone else's mannerisms
- 35  in an amusing and ironic way

**DOWN**
- 1  in a threatening way, indicating something bad is going to happen
- 2  in a humorless or formal manner
- 3  soothed; appeased; calmed
- 5  points of union; connections
- 6  fragments of something broken into pieces
- 8  moved in an exaggerated or angry way
- 9  critical or disparaging
- 12  clever and useful
- 13  with extreme anxiety or torment; distressed
- 16  thought deeply about
- 18  cringing or moving backward defensively in fear
- 19  abruptly, angrily, or bluntly in manner or speech
- 21  to seize and punish someone believed to have committed a crime
- 22  belligerent or aggressive in nature; quarrelsome
- 23  in a sorrowful or melancholy way; mournfully
- 26  thought carefully about someone or something; judged
- 27  moved clumsily or heavily
- 28  able to make decisions quickly; firm

Name _____ Period _____

## *Of Mice and Men*
## Vocabulary Review: Chapters 4-6

**ACROSS**
1. shook something abruptly
6. looked over; made a judgment about
8. in a clever or tricky way
12. grief or distress resulting from serious misfortune
13. turned away
14. behaved in a whining or self-pitying way
16. threw something with great force
18. responded in a witty, angry, or insulting manner
20. in an obedient manner; without protest
21. a pain-relieving cream or ointment
24. beat, battered, or tore at a person or animal
26. attempting to please with flattery
28. pulled away in a frightened manner
29. uninteresting or boring
30. wrapped or padded with material in order to stifle sound
31. struck at repeatedly; touched clumsily
32. uninvolved with people or events; remote
33. shouting or laughing at someone or something in a mocking or hurtful way
34. twisted or squirmed, especially from feelings of pain
35. provided comfort to someone who is distressed or saddened

**DOWN**
2. with negative judgment based upon personal standards
3. in a hostile, aggressive, or fighting manner
4. in a hostile, unsociable, or morose way
5. in an unrelentingly harsh or cruel way
7. feeling or expressing great contempt for someone or something
9. greatly bent out of shape
10. downcast, disappointed, or humiliated
11. in an emotionless, unresponsive manner
15. completely confused or puzzled
17. charming; friendly or trusting
19. an act or occasion of winning or being victorious
22. pierced with a sharp instrument
23. anger about an unfairness or wrongdoing
25. hip, buttocks, or upper thigh of an animal
27. moved swiftly and smoothly
29. unsatisfactorily small; unsatisfying

Name _____  Period _____

## *Of Mice and Men*
## Final Test

### Part A: Matching
**Directions**: Match the following characters with the correct description, action or quote. Write the letter of the correct answer on the line provided.

1. Lennie _____
2. George _____
3. Slim _____
4. the boss _____
5. Crooks _____
6. Candy _____
7. Curley _____
8. Curley's wife _____
9. Carlson _____

a. the first one to join Lennie and George's dream
b. a welterweight fighter
c. owned a Luger pistol
d. tells Lennie that he will go to the "booby hatch"
e. "Why do you got to get killed?  You ain't so little as mice."
f. suspicious of George's intentions
g. "Well I ain't giving you no trouble.  Think I don't like to talk to somebody ever' once in a while?"
h. "I ain't mad.  I never been mad, an' I ain't now."
i. "You hadda, George.  I swear you hadda."

### Part B: Multiple Choice
**Directions**: Write the letter of the best response on the line provided.

10. _____ The novel is set in:
    a. Tennessee          c. Alabama
    b. California          d. Oklahoma

11. _____ What is the name of the town George and Lennie left?
    a. Salinas            c. Weed
    b. Soledad            d. San Francisco

12. _____ What did Lennie want at dinner time?
    a. sausage            c. beans
    b. bread              d. ketchup

13. _____ How are George and Lennie different from the other migrant workers on the ranch?
    a. They have lots of money and have chosen to be migrant workers.
    b. They own a ranch together.
    c. They are related.
    d. They have a deep connection and friendship.

14. _____ What would have been Lennie's job on the ranch of their dreams?
    a. taking care of all the livestock      c. light farm work and general repairs
    b. tending the rabbits                   d. cooking the mens' meals

**Name** _____ **Period** _____

15. _____ When the boss first met George and Lennie, the boss was:
    a. proud and confident            c. frustrated and tired
    b. irritated and suspicious       d. excited and nervous

16. _____ The bunkhouses in which the men lived could be described as:
    a. sparse and dim                 c. open and airy
    b. dark and ornamented            d. personal and comfortable

17. _____ The old dog belonged to:
    a. Curley                         c. Candy
    b. Carlson                        d. Crooks

18. _____ Candy said that Curley picked a fight with Lennie because:
    a. Curley knew Lennie before      c. Curley doesn't like new guys
    b. Lennie flirted with Curley's wife  d. Curley doesn't like big guys

19. _____ Curley's wife could be described as:
    a. pretty, but reserved           c. pretty and shy
    b. lonely and flirtatious         d. pretty, but happily married

20. _____ What did George tell Lennie to do if he got in trouble?
    a. call the police                c. call him and the boss
    b. fight back                     d. run to the river

21. _____ Lennie and George left Weed because:
    a. Lennie raped a girl            c. Lennie stole money
    b. Lennie petted a girl's dress   d. the job was done

22. _____ Who shot the dog?
    a. Candy                          c. Carlson
    b. Slim                           d. Lennie

23. _____ Who was the second to want to join Lennie and George's dream, but then said he was only kidding about it?
    a. Candy                          c. Carlson
    b. Crooks                         d. Slim

24. _____ Which character does NOT suffer from loneliness?
    a. Candy                          c. Curley's wife
    b. Crooks                         d. George

25. _____ Crooks does not fit in with the other workers because he:
    a. doesn't want to                c. is segregated because of his race
    b. he doesn't know how to play cards  d. he is not liked by the other men

26. _____ How does Steinbeck foreshadow the death of Curley's wife?
    a. with the death of the puppy    c. with the accusation of rape
    b. with the death of the mouse Lennie carried  d. all of the above

Name _____  Period _____

27. _____ Why does George have to do all the talking for Lennie?
   a. George is smarter than Lennie.     c. Lennie might say the wrong thing.
   b. George is in charge of Lennie.     d. all of the above

28. _____ What era followed the Stock Market Crash of 1929?
   a. The Civil Rights Era      c. The Great Depression
   b. World War I               d. The Jazz Age

29. _____ What are Hoovervilles?
   a. the black Quarters            c. makeshift towns of very poor people
   b. big cities full of rich people   d. little communities within Weed

30. _____ Who introduced the *New Deal*?
   a. Herbert Hoover      c. Franklin Roosevelt
   b. John Steinbeck      d. Lennie Smalls

**Part C: Short Response**
*Directions: Answer the following questions using complete sentences on a separate piece of paper.*

31. Despite being slow, Lennie knew how to make George feel guilty. Describe two situations in which Lennie manipulated George and made him feel bad. What do these situations reveal about their relationship?

32. Steinbeck uses a lot of slang—even some curse words and foul language. Why do you think Steinbeck does this? What effect does the use of this language have on the way the story is told? How might the story be different if Steinbeck avoided this technique?

33. Using examples from the text, describe how the use of foreshadowing is used throughout the novel.

34. If you were a lawyer and Lennie was your client, how would you make your case for his innocence in the killing of Curley's wife? Justify your response with details and examples from the text leading up to the incident, as well as from the incident itself.

35. Do you agree or disagree with George's actions and the outcome of the novel? What is your opinion of the ending? What evidence would you cite to defend or criticize George's actions?

Name _____    Period _____

## Of Mice and Men
## Final Test: Vocabulary
*Chapters One and Two*

**Directions**: Match each vocabulary word in examples 1-9 with the correct definition or synonym from a-i.  Next, match each vocabulary word in examples 10-18 with the correct definition or synonym from j-r.  Write the letter of the correct answer on the line provided.

1. _____ junctures
2. _____ debris
3. _____ mottled
4. _____ lumbered
5. _____ brusquely
6. _____ pantomime
7. _____ contemplated
8. _____ anguished
9. _____ yammered

a. an imitation of someone else's mannerisms
b. with extreme anxiety or torment; distressed
c. points of union; connections
d. howled or wailed as if in pain; whimpered
e. thought deeply about
f. moved clumsily or heavily
g. spotted; marked with different colors
h. fragments of something broken into pieces
i. abruptly, angrily, or bluntly in manner or speech

10. _____ scoff (at)
11. _____ pugnacious
12. _____ gingerly
13. _____ handy
14. _____ ominously
15. _____ slough
16. _____ derogatory
17. _____ plaintively
18. _____ decisive

j. in a careful or cautious manner
k. in a threatening way, indicating something bad is going to happen
l. in a sorrowful or melancholy way; mournfully
m. belligerent or aggressive in nature; quarrelsome
n. able to make decisions quickly; firm
o. to cast something off; shed
p. critical or disparaging
q. to make fun of; tease
r. clever and useful

Name _____  Period _____

**Chapters Three and Four**

**Directions**: Match each vocabulary word in examples 19-27 with the correct definition or synonym from a-i. Next, match each vocabulary word in examples 28-36 with the correct definition or synonym from j-r. Write the letter of the correct answer on the line provided.

19. _____ derision
20. _____ lynch
21. _____ concealing
22. _____ stride
23. _____ gnawing
24. _____ entranced
25. _____ reprehensible
26. _____ bemused
27. _____ cowering

a. a long step
b. mocking scorn; ridicule
c. to seize and punish someone believed to have committed a crime
d. caused somebody to be confused or puzzled
e. cringing or moving backward defensively in fear
f. in a state of fascination or wonder
g. highly unacceptable; deserving criticism
h. persistent and troubling
i. putting or keeping someone or something out of sight; hiding

28. _____ solemnly
29. _____ mauled
30. _____ aloof
31. _____ meager
32. _____ brutally
33. _____ indignation
34. _____ averted
35. _____ appraised
36. _____ crestfallen

j. in an unrelentingly harsh or cruel way
k. looked over; made a judgment about
l. beat, battered, or tore at a person or animal
m. anger about an unfairness or wrongdoing
n. in a humorless or formal manner
o. downcast, disappointed, or humiliated
p. unsatisfactorily small; unsatisfying
q. uninvolved with people or events; remote
r. turned away

Name _____  Period _____

## Chapters Five and Six

**Directions:** Match each vocabulary word in examples 37-45 with the correct definition or synonym from a-i. Next, match each vocabulary word in examples 46-54 with the correct definition or synonym from j-r. Write the letter of the correct answer on the line provided.

37. _____ jeering
38. _____ hurled
39. _____ woe
40. _____ consoled
41. _____ contorted
42. _____ writhed
43. _____ muffled
44. _____ bewildered
45. _____ cringed

a. pulled away in a frightened manner
b. padded with material in order to stifle sound
c. completely confused or puzzled
d. greatly bent out of shape
e. grief or distress resulting from serious misfortune
f. threw something with great force
g. twisted or squirmed, especially from pain
h. shouting or laughing at someone or something in a mocking or hurtful way
i. provided comfort to someone who is distressed or saddened

46. _____ sniveled
47. _____ lanced
48. _____ retorted
49. _____ belligerently
50. _____ monotonous
51. _____ craftily
52. _____ triumph
53. _____ dutifully
54. _____ jarred

j. pierced with a sharp instrument
k. in a hostile, aggressive, or fighting manner
l. in a clever or tricky way
m. responded in a witty, angry, or insulting manner
n. shook something abruptly
o. in an obedient manner; without protest
p. behaved in a whining or self-pitying way
q. an act or occasion of winning or being victorious
r. uninteresting or boring

Name _____   Period _____

## Of Mice and Men
## Final Test: Multiple Choice

*Directions*: On your answer document, fill in the bubble of the correct response.

### Part A: Reading

1. Who tells Lennie that he will go to the "booby hatch"?
   a. Crooks
   b. Candy
   c. Carlson
   d. Curley's Wife
2. Who was the first one to join Lennie and George's dream?
   a. Crooks
   b. Candy
   c. Slim
   d. Carlson
3. Who was a welterweight fighter?
   a. Carlson
   b. Slim
   c. Candy
   d. Curley
4. Who owned a Luger pistol?
   a. the boss
   b. Candy
   c. Carlson
   d. Crooks
5. Who said "Why do you got to get killed? You ain't so little as mice"?
   a. Curley's Wife
   b. Carlson
   c. Lennie
   d. George
6. Who said "Well I ain't giving you no trouble. Think I don't like to talk to somebody ever' once in a while?"
   a. Candy
   b. Curley's Wife
   c. Crooks
   d. Lennie
7. Who said "I ain't mad. I never been mad, an' I ain't now"?
   a. George
   b. Slim
   c. Carlson
   d. Crooks
8. Who said "You hadda, George. I swear you hadda"?
   a. George
   b. Slim
   c. Carlson
   d. Crooks
9. Who said "Whatever we ain't got, that's what you want"?
   a. Crooks
   b. George
   c. Lennie
   d. Curley's Wife
10. Who said "S'pose you couldn't go into the bunk house and play rummy 'cause you was black"?
    a. Crooks
    b. George
    c. Lennie
    d. Curley's Wife
11. The novel is set in:
    a. Tennessee
    b. Alabama
    c. California
    d. Virginia
12. What is the name of the town George and Lennie left?
    a. Salinas
    b. Weed
    c. Soledad
    d. San Francisco
13. What did Lennie want at dinner time?
    a. sausage
    b. beans
    c. bread
    d. ketchup
14. How are George and Lennie different from the other migrant workers on the ranch?
    a. They have lots of money and have chosen to be migrant workers.
    b. They own a ranch together.
    c. They are related.
    d. They have a deep connection and friendship.

©2009 Secondary Solutions

Name _____   Period _____

15. What would have been Lennie's job on the ranch of their dreams?
    a. taking care of all the livestock
    b. light farm work and general repairs
    c. tending the rabbits
    d. cooking the mens' meals
16. When the boss first met George and Lennie, the boss was:
    a. proud and confident
    b. frustrated and tired
    c. irritated and suspicious
    d. excited and nervous
17. The bunkhouses in which the men lived could be described as:
    a. sparse and dim
    b. open and airy
    c. dark and ornamented
    d. personal and comfortable
18. The old dog belonged to:
    a. Curley
    b. Candy
    c. Carlson
    d. Crooks
19. Candy said that Curley picked a fight with Lennie because:
    a. Curley knew Lennie before
    b. Curley didn't like new guys
    c. Lennie flirted with Curley's wife
    d. Curley didn't like big guys
20. Curley's wife could be described as:
    a. pretty, but reserved
    b. lonely and flirtatious
    c. pretty and shy
    d. pretty, but happily married
21. What did George tell Lennie to do if he got in trouble?
    a. call the police
    b. call him and the boss
    c. fight back
    d. run to the river
22. Lennie and George left Weed because:
    a. Lennie raped a girl
    b. Lennie stole money
    c. Lennie petted a girl's dress
    d. The job was done

23. Who was the second to want to join Lennie and George's dream, but then said he was only joking?
    a. Candy
    b. Carlson
    c. Crooks
    d. Slim
24. Which character does NOT suffer from loneliness?
    a. Candy
    b. Curley's wife
    c. Crooks
    d. George
25. Crooks does not fit in with the other workers because he:
    a. doesn't want to
    b. is segregated because of his race
    c. doesn't know how to play cards
    d. is not liked by the other men
26. How does Steinbeck foreshadow the death of Curley's wife?
    a. with the death of the puppy
    b. with the accusation of rape
    c. with the death of the mouse Lennie carried
    d. all of the above
27. Why does George have to do all the talking for Lennie?
    a. George is smarter than Lennie.
    b. Lennie might say the wrong thing.
    c. George is in charge of Lennie.
    d. all of the above
28. What era followed the Stock Market Crash of 1929?
    a. The Civil Rights Era
    b. The Great Depression
    c. World War I
    d. The Jazz Age
29. What are Hoovervilles?
    a. makeshift towns of very poor people
    b. the black quarters
    c. big cities full of rich people
    d. little communities within Weed
30. Who introduced the *New Deal*?
    a. Herbert Hoover
    b. Franklin Roosevelt
    c. John Steinbeck
    d. Lennie Smalls

**Name** _____  **Period** _____

## Part B: Short Response
***Directions****: Answer the following questions using complete sentences on a separate piece of paper.*

31. Despite being slow, Lennie knew how to make George feel guilty. Describe two situations in which Lennie manipulated George and made him feel bad. What do these situations reveal about their relationship?

32. Steinbeck uses a lot of slang—even some curse words and foul language. Why do you think Steinbeck does this? What effect does the use of this language have on the way the story is told? How might the story be different if Steinbeck avoided this technique?

33. Using examples from the text, describe how the use of foreshadowing is used throughout the novel.

34. If you were a lawyer and Lennie was your client, how would you make your case for his innocence in the killing of Curley's wife? Justify your response with details and examples from the text leading up to the incident, as well as from the incident itself.

35. Do you agree or disagree with George's actions and the outcome of the novel? What is your opinion of the ending? What evidence would you cite to defend or criticize George's actions?

# *Of Mice and Men* Teacher Guide
*Summary of the Novel*

A simple, yet poignant story of friendship, hope and dreams, *Of Mice and Men* is arguably one of John Steinbeck's greatest works. Set in California in the 1930s Depression Era, the story begins as two men, George, tough but likeable, and Lennie, a large, lumbering man with mental deficiencies, find their way along the Salinas River. They have come from Weed, where Lennie was accused of raping a girl. As the men make camp for the night, we learn more about George and Lennie's relationship, and understand quickly that although George complains about having to take care of Lennie, he knows he needs Lennie's companionship and friendship. It is in the first chapter that we learn of their dream of owning and running a farm together, where Lennie can tend the rabbits, and they both can *"live off the fatta the lan'."*

The next morning, George and Lennie arrive at their new job. George has told Lennie to keep his mouth shut, and that he would do all the talking. Because of this, the boss becomes immediately suspicious of their relationship, and warns George not to cause trouble. As the men find their way around the bunkhouse, a small, fiery man named Curley interrupts. He immediately picks a fight with Lennie, and after he leaves, the old swamper, Candy, warns the men about Curley's temper and history of fighting, as well as about Curley's new wife, whom he describes as a "tart."

Later that evening, Lennie excitedly plays with the new puppy Slim, the jerkline skinner has given him. As George and Slim get to know each other, George realizes he can trust Slim, and confides in him their trouble in Weed, and why they were on the run. He reveals that Lennie never means to hurt anyone, and that he was just trying to pet the girl's dress, but that he held on and scared the girl. She went running for help, and accused him of trying to rape her. After they play cards and talk for awhile, Slim leaves and Lennie and George are left alone. Lennie asks to hear the dream again, so George tells the story, unaware that Candy is listening all along. Enthralled by the idea, Candy offers money he has saved to become a part of George and Lennie's plan to own a farm. George gets excited at the prospect of the dream actually becoming a reality, and welcomes Candy to the "dream." The peace and excitement is interrupted again, however, when Curley rushes in, looking for Slim. Thinking about the plans in motion, Lennie cannot contain his enthusiasm. Curley misconstrues his smiling face, and accuses Lennie of making fun of him. He punches Lennie in the face, and with George's consent, Lennie fights back, crushing Curley's hand. Slim warns Curley to keep his mouth shut about the incident, admonishing him to tell others that he caught his hand in a machine.

The next evening, the men go to town to relax and unwind. Lennie, left behind, wanders into the barn to see his puppy, but is curious about the room in the barn which is inhabited by Crooks, the black stable hand. Even though Crooks is unfriendly and detached, Lennie tries to strike up a conversation. Crooks's veneer begins to crack, and they get to know a bit about each other. Looking for Lennie, Candy comes by and joins the men. Crooks learns of the dream, and while he initially scoffs at the idea, he realizes the possibility, and offers an extra hand to get in on the plan too. Curley's wife saunters in, and is treated coldly by the men. She becomes angry at their rudeness, and threatens Crooks. Finally, thinking the other men have returned, she leaves. George comes in to get Lennie, and they leave. Candy and Crooks are left alone, and Crooks backs out on the deal, telling Candy he was never serious about joining them.

Chapter Five opens as Lennie sits cradling and petting his dead puppy. He was too rough with the puppy, and ended up breaking his neck. He is mad and scared, and worries that George will never allow him to tend the rabbits once George sees what he has done. Curley's wife reappears and sees Lennie with the dead puppy. She talks with him about her loneliness and about dreams of becoming an actress. After Lennie confesses he likes to pet soft things, and that is how the puppy died, Curley's wife says that she understands and invites Lennie to feel her soft hair. He does, and gets so excited that he doesn't let go when she struggles, and ends up breaking her neck, killing her. Knowing that he has done a "bad thing," Lennie runs away to the spot by the river. Candy comes into the barn and sees Curley's wife, dead, and immediately runs for George. Both George and Candy know that Lennie is responsible. Not wanting to be accused of being an accomplice, George goes back to the bunkhouse as Candy tells the other men about Curley's wife. Curley immediately assumes Lennie is responsible, and goes after him. The other men go along to help.

Meanwhile, by telling the men that Lennie went another direction, George buys himself and Lennie more time, and he runs to the river's edge, where they had agreed to meet if there should be any trouble. Before George arrives, Lennie sees images of his Aunt Clara and a giant rabbit, taunting him. George arrives and tries to calm and console Lennie. As he retells the story of the dream, and reassures Lennie that he is not mad at him, George shoots Lennie in the back of the head, killing him. The other men arrive, and only Slim understands the truth of what has transpired. He reassures George, telling him he "hadda" do it.

# Of Mice and Men
*Vocabulary with Definitions*

**Chapter One**
1. **junctures**: noun; points of union; connections
2. **debris**: noun; fragments of something broken into pieces
3. **mottled**: adj.; spotted; marked with different colors
4. **recumbent**: adj.; lying back; resting or leaning
5. **morosely**: adv.; in a withdrawn or gloomy way; sadly; thoughtfully
6. **lumbered**: verb.; moved clumsily or heavily
7. **brusquely**: adv.; abruptly, angrily, or bluntly in manner or speech
8. **pantomime**: noun; an imitation of someone else's mannerisms
9. **contemplated**: verb; thought deeply about
10. **imperiously**: adv.; in a haughty, dictatorial, or overbearing manner
11. **anguished**: adj.; with extreme anxiety or torment; distressed
12. **yammered**: verb; howled or wailed as if in pain; whimpered

**Chapter Two**
1. **scoff** (at): verb; to make fun of; tease
2. **mollified**: adj.; soothed, appeased; calmed
3. **pugnacious**: adj.; belligerent or aggressive in nature; quarrelsome
4. **gingerly**: adv.; very carefully
5. **handy**: adj.; clever and useful
6. **ominously**: adv.; in a threatening way, indicating something bad is going to happen
7. **slough**: verb; to cast something off; shed
8. **derogatory**: adj.; critical or disparaging
9. **flounced**: verb; moved in an exaggerated or angry way
10. **plaintively**: adv.; in a sorrowful or melancholy way; mournfully
11. **decisive**: adj.; able to make decisions quickly; firm
12. **complacently**: adv.; with self-satisfaction; smugly

**Chapter Three**
1. **derision**: noun; mocking scorn; ridicule
2. **lynch**: verb; to seize and punish someone believed to have committed a crime
3. **concealing**: verb; putting or keeping someone or something out of sight; hiding
4. **stride**: noun; a long step
5. **gnawing**: adj.; persistent and troubling
6. **entranced**: verb; in a state of fascination or wonder
7. **reprehensible**: adj.; highly unacceptable; deserving criticism
8. **bemused**: adj.; caused somebody to be confused or puzzled
9. **cowering**: verb; cringing or moving backward defensively in fear
10. **regarded**: verb; thought carefully about someone or something; judged
11. **wryly**: adv.; in an amusing and ironic way
12. **solemnly**: adv.; in a humorless or formal manner

**Chapter Four**
1. **mauled**: verb; beat, battered, or tore at a person or animal
2. **aloof**: adj.; uninvolved with people or events; remote
3. **meager**: adj.; unsatisfactorily small; unsatisfying
4. **liniment**: noun; a pain-relieving cream or ointment
5. **fawning**: adj.; attempting to please with flattery
6. **disarming**: adj.; charming; friendly or trusting
7. **scornful**: adj.; feeling or expressing great contempt for someone or something
8. **brutally**: adv.; in an unrelentingly harsh or cruel way
9. **indignation**: noun; anger about an unfairness or wrongdoing
10. **averted**: verb; turned away

Name _____   Period _____

11. **appraised**: verb; looked over; made a judgment about
12. **crestfallen**: adj.; downcast, disappointed, or humiliated

**Chapter Five**
1. **jeering**: (participle; adj.); shouting or laughing at someone or something in a mocking or hurtful way
2. **hurled**: verb; threw something with great force
3. **sullenly**: adv; in a hostile, unsociable, or morose way
4. **woe**: noun; grief or distress resulting from serious misfortune
5. **consoled**: verb; provided comfort to someone who is distressed or saddened
6. **contorted**: verb; greatly bent out of shape
7. **writhed**: verb; twisted or squirmed, especially from feelings of pain
8. **muffled**: adj.; wrapped or padded with material in order to stifle sound
9. **bewildered**: adj.; completely confused or puzzled
10. **pawed**: verb; struck at repeatedly; touched clumsily
11. **cringed**: verb; pulled away in a frightened manner
12. **sniveled**: verb; behaved in a whining or self-pitying way

**Chapter Six**
1. **lanced**: verb; pierced with a sharp instrument
2. **scudded**: verb; moved swiftly and smoothly
3. **disapprovingly**: adv.; with negative judgment based upon personal standards
4. **haunches**: noun; hip, buttocks, or upper thigh of an animal
5. **retorted**: verb; responded in a witty, angry, or insulting manner
6. **belligerently**: adv.; in a hostile, aggressive, or fighting manner
7. **woodenly**: adv.; in an emotionless, unresponsive manner; like wood
8. **monotonous**: adj., uninteresting or boring
9. **craftily**: adv.; in a clever or tricky way
10. **triumph**: noun; an act or occasion of winning or being victorious
11. **dutifully**: adv., in an obedient manner; without protest
12. **jarred**: verb; shook something abruptly

*Definitions and parts of speech of vocabulary words are given as the word is used in context.*

## Pre-Reading Activities
Suggested activities prior to the study of *Of Mice and Men*:

1. Have students journal/discuss the concept of having dreams and goals for the future. Are dreams and goals important? What happens when those dreams are not fulfilled? What if other people make fun of or doubt those dreams? Is it more important to look at reality or to have dreams? Can you do both?
2. Steinbeck uses very descriptive language to create a vivid and realistic setting. Have students read the first two paragraphs of Chapter One. Then break the students up into 5 small groups. Assign each group a different sense: touch, taste, sight, hearing, smell. Have the groups reread the paragraphs, finding as many sensory details for their sense as they can. (The groups with taste and smell will have a more difficult time.) After 3 to 5 minutes, rotate senses and have them do the same thing. Keep rotating until every group has found details for each sense. After they have finished, discuss the effect of the sensory details on the mood and comprehension of the reader.
3. Have students research the economic and political concerns regarding the Great Depression. Choose from President Hoover, President Roosevelt, Wall Street, "New Deal," Social Security, rumors of Hitler, etc. Have them compile the information in a brochure, poster, or computer presentation, complete with appropriate photos.
4. Have students research the trends of the 1930s, including music, theater, movies, literature, fashion, etc. Have them compile the information in a poster, computer presentation, or newspaper, complete with advertisements, weather predictions, photos, classified ads, announcements, etc. Allow at least three days for in-class activity.
5. Have students find 5-10 photographs taken during The Great Depression. Have them create a poster or collage of the photographs. Have them choose the one photo that affected them the most, and have them write a paragraph or poem illustrating why they chose that particular photo, who they think the people are, where they are from, and what they think the photo is depicting.
6. Have students act as "expert groups" on the following topics of research: The Dust Bowl, The Great Depression, Hoovervilles, Migrant Workers, The New Deal, the Stock Market Crash of 1929, California in the 1930s, Agriculture of California, the Works Progress Administration, and the Federal Writer's Project and have these expert groups make presentations or Webquests on their topic.

## Post-Reading Activities and Alternative Assessment
*Suggested activities to supplement the study of **Of Mice and Men** after reading the novel:*

**Cross-Curricular Activities (Multiple Subjects)**
1. Create an informative poster or brochure about mental retardation, including facts and statistics about the disability, characteristics, treatment, challenges, adaptive skills, and related laws.
2. Create a new book jacket for the novel. The book jacket must have a picture that represents the novel on the front cover, and a summary of the novel on the back cover. Other elements, such as critics' reviews and an author biography and photo will earn additional points.
3. Create a shoebox diorama of the ranchers' bunkhouse or the barn where Lennie slept with the puppy. Include as many accurate details as possible.
4. Create a newspaper of the day George shot Lennie. Include as many details of the event as possible in the main article. Also include advertisements, horoscopes, photos, gossip and advice columns, letters to the editor, or other newsworthy events to enhance the project.
5. Design and draw appropriate costumes for each of the main characters in the novel. Include drawings for Lennie, George, Curley, Curley's wife, and Slim. Attach fabric swatches and include a short description of the costume, including the scene(s) in which the character would be dressed in the costume.
6. Cast your own film or stage version of *Of Mice and Men*. First, using popular celebrities of today, cast the roles of each of the characters in the play. Remember—they must fit the character! Then, create a theater program or movie poster announcing the opening night of your version of *Of Mice and Men*, including the names of the stars and which parts they play, the dates and times of the performances, a brief summary of the novel, and an eye-catching picture to bring in the audience.
7. Create a poster or brochure on the life and work of John Steinbeck. Include information about major events in his life, his major works, and how his life is related to his novels and short stories.
8. Create a Cause and Effect diagram, explaining how each event of the book caused other events to occur. What might have happened had one of the events not occurred? Choose an event to change, and rewrite the events that occurred because of that change.

**Science/Technology**
1. Create a presentation about science, technology, and new inventions of the Depression era. Include research on: invention of radio, plastics, nylon stockings, Charles Lindbergh, electron microscope, early air conditioners and refrigerators, rubber wheels, neutron discovery, Hoover Dam, Golden Gate Bridge, and/or the 1933 World's Fair.
2. Use the Internet to compile an annotated list of helpful websites related to *Of Mice and Men*. Find sites about the author and the novel itself, plus sites about The Great Depression, The Dust Bowl, Migrant Workers, etc.

**Art/Music**
1. Use a computer program or draw/paint an original CD cover depicting one of the themes from *Of Mice and Men*. On your CD, include a compilation of 15 songs (both new and old) you feel best represent the most important scenes of the novel. Put together a report of your songs, including the name of the song, artist, and album the song came from, a copy of the lyrics, and a minimum one paragraph explanation of why you chose each song to represent a particular theme, and which event or incident the song represents. For example, you may choose a specific song for when Candy's dog is taken out to be shot. What song would be appropriate to represent the mood during this scene? Why?

2. Compare and contrast the book and the movie version of *Of Mice and Men* starring Gary Sinise. What do you think about the cast of characters? What do you think about the direction, such as the decision to leave parts of the book out, or to add scenes to the film? How well did the director capture the important themes and ideas of the novel?
3. Create a board game which includes the following:
    a. Game Cards (at least 20) which contain quotations from *Of Mice and Men*; include the name of the speaker of the quote somewhere on the card.
    b. Game Pieces (4-8 different ones) representing the characters in *Of Mice and Men*.
    c. Game Board complete with your art work, which relates to *Of Mice and Men*.
    d. Typed directions on how to play the game, the object of the game, and how to win. Have some friends or classmates "test-play" your game.
4. Create a 20-25 page children's book of *Of Mice and Men*. Using large, easy to read font and short, elementary-level words and sentences, tell about the story's important events and characters, making sure the themes come across to the reader. Include pictures that depict the story.

**Social Science/History**
1. Participate in a debate of Lennie's innocence or guilt in the death of Curley's wife. Should he have been put on trial? Was he guilty or innocent? Use evidence from the text to support arguments for each side.
2. Create a presentation about women of the 1930s, including fashion, careers, family, work, church, and social obligations. You may also choose to include research on famous women of the era such as Eleanor Roosevelt, Mary McLeod Bethune, Gertrude Stein, Frances Perkins, Georgia O'Keeffe, Bette Davis, Greta Garbo, Margaret Mitchell, Pearl S. Buck, Amelia Earhart, Dorothea Lange, Agatha Christie, and/or Mildred "Babe" Didrikson.
3. Create a presentation of famous black Americans of the 1930s such as George Washington Carver, Jesse Owens, Jackie Robinson, W.E.B. Du Bois, Mary McLeod Bethune, Zora Neale Hurston, Langston Hughes, Charles Drew, Duke Ellington, Benny Goodman, Hattie McDaniel, James Weldon Johnson, Countee Cullen, Eugene Toomer, Sterling Brown, and/or Claude McKay.
4. Create a presentation on the economic and political concerns of the 1930s, including The New Deal, Dust Bowl, Hoover, Roosevelt, Social Security, the WPA, Wall Street, Hitler, Stalin, the League of Nations, and Winston Churchill. Include statistics on the U.S. population, average salary, and cost of living, including home, rent, car, etc.
5. Create a presentation of daily life during the Depression. Some ideas to include: plastic, nylon stockings, lawn tennis, stamp collecting, Baseball Hall of Fame, Howard Hughes, Lindbergh kidnapping, 21$^{st}$ amendment, Empire State Building, Monopoly, radio, riding the rails, Tarzan, comics Laurel and Hardy, Dick and Jane books, and/or the Harlem Renaissance.

**Mathematics**
1. Research the cost of living in the 1930s during the Great Depression, comparing and contrasting your findings with the cost of living today. How much has the cost of living increased or decreased? What is the change in the average salary? What is the population increase in the U.S.? What percentages are unemployed? What is the national debt, in comparison? Be sure to compare common items including the cost of a new home, a new car, a refrigerator, loaf of bread, gallon of milk, etc. from the 30s and today, and then compare them to the average salary. Create a graph to include with your findings.

## Essay Ideas

*For this Guide, essay and writing activities are two different types of writing assignments. On this page are essay assignments. For the essay ideas, be sure to answer the questions in a succinct, comprehensive, five-paragraph essay. Each answer should be at least 2-3 typed, double-spaced pages.*

1. Analyze George's role in the novel. Consider his role as a worker, caretaker, as well as a friend to Lennie. How does he change throughout the novel?
2. Compare and contrast George and Lennie. In what ways are they alike? Different? How might the story have been different if Lennie was not mentally deficient?
3. The killing of Candy's old dog was significant on several levels. Discuss the significance of the killing, including the concept of old age and worth, and the foreshadowing of Lennie's death. Include any similarities or differences between the death of Candy's dog and Lennie's death.
4. The concept of "having someone" weaves throughout the novel. Discuss the significance of this idea, along with the theme of loneliness. Be sure to include observations about the "outcasts" on the ranch, including Lennie, Crooks, Candy, and Curley's wife.
5. Write about what you would have done in the same situation, if you had been one of the characters in *Of Mice and Men*. Be sure to include the name of the character, the situation from the novel that you would have handled differently, and how you would have handled it.
6. Steinbeck was going to name his story "Something That Happened." Instead, he named if *Of Mice and Men.* Which title do you think is more appropriate to the novel? Explain your answer.
7. Analyze Steinbeck's portrayal of Curley's wife as the lone female on the all-male ranch.
8. *Of Mice and Men* is one of the top 10 most challenged books in schools since 1990, according to the American Library Association. Should the book be banned in schools? Why or why not? Use textual examples to support your response.
9. Select what you consider the most important episode in *Of Mice and Men*. Why do you feel this is so important? Explain what happened and how you feel this incident or situation affected the novel as a whole.
10. What changes would you suggest for *Of Mice and Men*? What appealed and didn't appeal to you in the novel? Make suggestions for change, explain why you would make the changes, and explain how these changes would improve the novel.

## Writing Ideas

1. Write a journal from George's point of view about George and Lennie's adventures. A minimum of ten entries should be included in the journal. Entries should focus on major events in the character's life and how he would respond to each event. Remember—*you are George* while you are writing in this diary; the written dialect is desirable, but not mandatory. Finally, create a unique cover for the diary.
2. Conduct an interview with Lennie, George, Slim or any other character of your choice from the novel. Write 10 questions that will give the character a chance to tell his or her story about a specific incident from his or her point of view. You may ask questions, challenge a situation, express a complaint, or make a suggestion. Then answer the questions in the persona of the character you chose, using insight into the character and details from the story to support your response.
3. Conduct a personal interview with someone who lived during the Great Depression. Be sure to prepare no less than ten questions before the interview, then write a report of the information you gathered from this first-person perspective.
4. Write a different ending for the story. What if George had not killed Lennie? What if Curley had reached Lennie first? What if Lennie had been arrested and put on trial? You choose from where the story changes.
5. Write a "what if" situation. For example, what if Lennie had not killed Curley's Wife? What if George had not shot Lennie? Create an alternate situation, changing the appropriate events and outcome of the story to reflect your "what if" question.
6. Write a letter to a friend or family member reviewing *Of Mice and Men*. Be sure to use correct letter format and include information about characters, a short summary, explanation of themes, and your opinion of the book.
7. Gather and analyze two more poems by Robert Burns or a writer of the Depression Era, such as Harlem Renaissance poets Langston Hughes, Richard Wright, Zora Neale Hurston, Ralph Ellison, Claude McKay, Margaret Walker, Willard Motley, and Frank Yerby, or others such as the Auden Group, John Wheelwright, William Butler Yeats, Louis Zukofsky, George Oppen, or writers who contributed to the Federal Writers' Project.
8. Write a 10-20 line poem expressing one of the themes of the novel and/or your personal perspective or feelings about the novel.
9. If given the opportunity, what questions would you like to ask John Steinbeck? Write a list of 10 questions you would ask him about his novel or life and explain why you chose those particular questions to ask him.
10. You are a psychologist, and your patient is a character of your choice from *Of Mice and Men*. He or she has come seeking advice. What questions would you ask your patient? What advice would you give? Compose notes and/or a tape recording of your thoughts during and/or after a "session." Also consider dream analysis and role-playing exercises. You must have at least five consecutive sessions and include a final diagnosis/recommendation for your patient.
11. Add a new character to *Of Mice and Men*. Describe your character. What would he or she contribute to the plot? Consider adding dialogue in the appropriate places within the novel.

*Project Rubric A*

| Category | Score of 5 | Score of 4 | Score of 3 | Score of 2 | Score of 1 | Score |
|---|---|---|---|---|---|---|
| **Required Elements** | Includes all of the required elements as stated in the directions. | Includes all but one or two of the required elements as stated in the directions. | Missing 3 or 4 of the required elements as stated in the directions. | Missing 5 or 6 of the required elements as stated in the directions. | Project does not follow the directions. | |
| **Graphics, Pictures** | All pictures, drawings, or graphics are appropriate, and add to the enjoyment of the project. | Some pictures, drawings, or graphics are included, are appropriate, and add to the enjoyment of the project. | A few pictures, drawings, or graphics are included and are appropriate to the project. | A few pictures, drawings, or graphics are included, but may not be appropriate to the project, or may be distracting. | Pictures or drawings are not used and/or are inappropriate or distracting to the project. | |
| **Creativity** | Exceptionally clever and unique; design and presentation enhance the project. | Clever at times; thoughtfully and uniquely presented. | A few original or clever touches enhance the project. | Little evidence of uniqueness, individuality, and/or effort. | No evidence of creativity or effort. Project is not unique. | |
| **Neatness, Appeal** | Exceptionally neat and attractive; typed or very neatly hand-written, appropriate use of color, particularly neat in design and layout. | Neat and attractive; typed or neatly hand-written, good use of color, good design and layout. | Generally neat and attractive; hand-written, some use of color, some problems in design and layout. | Distractingly messy or disorganized; hand-written; little use of color; several problems in design and layout. | Work shows no pride or effort. Project is incomplete, illegible, or particularly messy and unattractive. | |
| **Grammar, Spelling, Mechanics** | Little to no problems with grammar, spelling, and mechanics. Project was clearly proofread. | A few problems with grammar, spelling, or mechanics. Errors are minor and do not distract from the project. | Several errors in grammar, spelling, or mechanics. Errors can be slightly distracting at times. | Several problems with grammar, spelling, or mechanics. Errors are distracting. | Many problems with grammar, spelling, or mechanics. Mistakes clearly show project was not proofread. | |

Comments:

Final Score: _____ out of 25

*Project Rubric B*

| Category | Score of 5 | Score of 4 | Score of 3 | Score of 2 | Score of 1 | Score |
|---|---|---|---|---|---|---|
| **Required Elements** | Includes all of the required elements as stated in the directions. | Includes all but one or two of the required elements as stated in the directions. | Missing 3 or 4 of the required elements as stated in the directions. | Missing 5 or 6 of the required elements as stated in the directions. | Project does not follow the directions. | |
| **Creativity** | Exceptionally clever and unique; design and presentation enhance the project. | Clever at times; thoughtfully and uniquely presented. | A few original or clever touches enhance the project. | Little evidence of uniqueness, individuality, and/or effort. | No evidence of creativity or effort. Project is not unique. | |
| **Neatness, Appeal** | Exceptionally neat and attractive; typed or very neatly hand-written, appropriate use of color, particularly neat in design and layout. | Neat and attractive; typed or neatly hand-written, good use of color, good design and layout. | Generally neat and attractive; hand-written, some use of color, some problems in design and layout. | Distractingly messy or disorganized; hand-written; little use of color; several problems in design and layout. | Work shows no pride or effort. Project is incomplete, illegible, or particularly messy and unattractive. | |
| **Grammar, Spelling, Mechanics** | Little to no problems with grammar, spelling, and mechanics. Project was clearly proofread. | A few problems with grammar, spelling, or mechanics. Errors are minor and do not distract from the project. | Several errors in grammar, spelling, or mechanics. Errors can be slightly distracting at times. | Several problems with grammar, spelling, or mechanics. Errors are distracting. | Many problems with grammar, spelling, or mechanics. Mistakes clearly show project was not proofread. | |
| **Citation of Sources** | All graphics, pictures, and written work are original, or if they have been obtained from an outside source, have been properly cited. | All graphics, pictures, and written work that are not original or have been obtained from an outside source have been cited, with a few problems. | All graphics, pictures, and written work that are not original or have been obtained from an outside source have been cited, with several problems. | Some attempt has been made to give credit for unoriginal graphics, pictures, and written work. | No attempt has been made to give credit for unoriginal graphics, pictures, and written work. | |

**Comments:**

**Final Score:** _____ out of 25

*Response to Literature Rubric*

## Adapted from the **California Writing Assessment Rubric**
California Department of Education, Standards and Assessment Division

# Score of 4
- ☐ Clearly addresses all parts of the writing task.
- ☐ Provides a meaningful thesis and thoughtfully supports the thesis and main ideas with facts, details, and/or explanations.
- ☐ Maintains a consistent tone and focus and a clear sense of purpose and audience.
- ☐ Illustrates control in organization, including effective use of transitions.
- ☐ Provides a variety of sentence types and uses precise, descriptive language.
- ☐ Contains few, if any, errors in the conventions of the English language (grammar, punctuation, capitalization, spelling). These errors do not interfere with the reader's understanding of the writing.
- ☐ Demonstrates a *clear* understanding of the ambiguities, nuances, and complexities of the text.
- ☐ Develops interpretations that demonstrate a thoughtful, comprehensive, insightful grasp of the text, and supports these judgments with specific references to various texts.
- ☐ Draws well-supported inferences about the effects of a literary work on its audience.
- ☐ Provides *specific* textual examples and/or personal knowledge and details to support the interpretations and inferences.

# Score of 3
- ☐ Addresses all parts of the writing task.
- ☐ Provides a thesis and supports the thesis and main ideas with mostly relevant facts, details, and/or explanations.
- ☐ Maintains a generally consistent tone and focus and a general sense of purpose and audience.
- ☐ Illustrates control in organization, including *some* use of transitions.
- ☐ Includes a variety of sentence types and *some* descriptive language.
- ☐ Contains some errors in the conventions of the English language. These errors do not interfere with the reader's understanding of the writing.
- ☐ Develops interpretations that demonstrate a comprehensive grasp of the text and supports these interpretations with references to various texts.
- ☐ Draws supported inferences about the effects of a literary work on its audience.
- ☐ Supports judgments with some specific references to various texts and/or personal knowledge.
- ☐ Provides textual examples and details to support the interpretations.

## Score of 2
- ☐ Addresses *only parts* of the writing task.
- ☐ *Suggests* a central idea with *limited* facts, details, and/or explanation.
- ☐ Demonstrates *little* understanding of purpose and audience.
- ☐ Maintains an *inconsistent* point of view, focus, and/or organizational structure which may include *ineffective or awkward* transitions that do not unify important ideas.
- ☐ Contains *several errors* in the conventions of the English language. These errors may interfere with the reader's understanding of the writing.
- ☐ Develops interpretations that demonstrate a limited grasp of the text.
- ☐ Includes interpretations that *lack* accuracy or coherence as related to ideas, premises, or images from the literary work.
- ☐ Draws *few* inferences about the effects of a literary work on its audience.
- ☐ Supports judgments with *few, if any*, references to various text and/or personal knowledge.

## Score of 1
- ☐ Addresses *only one* part of the writing task.
- ☐ *Lacks* a thesis or central idea but may contain *marginally related* facts, details, and/or explanations.
- ☐ Demonstrates *no* understanding of purpose and audience.
- ☐ *Lacks* a clear point of view, focus, organizational structure, and transitions that unify important ideas.
- ☐ Includes *no* sentence variety; sentences are simple.
- ☐ Contains *serious errors* in the conventions of the English language. These errors interfere with the reader's understanding of the writing.
- ☐ Develops interpretations that demonstrate *little* grasp of the text.
- ☐ *Lacks* an interpretation or *may* be a simple retelling of the text.
- ☐ *Lacks* inferences about the effects of a literary work on its audience.
- ☐ *Fails* to support judgments with references to various text and/or personal knowledge.
- ☐ *Lacks* textual examples and details.

# Answer Key

*Note: Answers may not be given in complete sentences, as most student answers should be.*

**Page 11: Comprehension Check: Author Biography**
1. *Cup of Gold* (1929), *Tortilla Flat* (1935), *Of Mice and Men* (1937), *The Grapes of Wrath* (1939), *Sea of Cortez* (1941), *The Forgotten Village* (1941), *Cannery Row*, (1945), *East of Eden* (1951), *The Winter of Our Discontent* (1961)
2. *Of Mice and Men* was conceived as a play; won the Drama Critics Circle Award and the Pulitzer Prize in 1937. *The Grapes of Wrath* received harsh criticism, but the general public loved it; won the Pulitzer in 1940.
3. Born in 1902 in Salinas, CA. Father—John Ernst, Mother—Olive Hamilton; He liked to read and write; at 14 tried to translate *Le Morte d'Arthur*; went to Stanford, but did not graduate; married Carol in 1930; had friend Ed Ricketts; divorced Carol in 1943, married Gwendolyn; had two sons; divorced in 1948; married Elaine Scott in 1950.
4. Ability to capture the human spirit; captured the bleak, but realistic side of life; empathetic with life during the Depression; captured all the glory and cruelty of life; platform for social and political issues. *Answers will vary.*
5. *Answers will vary.*
6. *Timelines will vary.*

**Page 13: Comprehension Check: The Great Depression**
1. indisputable—not to be questioned; impossible to doubt; unprecedented—having no parallel or equivalent; bankruptcy—legal inability to pay debts; the state of having been legally declared bankrupt; stagnation—being undeveloped, unable to make progress, or unable to change
2. America was experiencing a time of great prosperity and living a life of excess; people had a lot of money and weren't afraid to spend it; people had credit cards, and were spending more than they made.
3. The stock market began to crash and money lost its worth; people began to lose their jobs and couldn't afford things anymore
4. Because people couldn't afford food, production of new crops slowed. Demand went down, so supply decreased in response.
5. Banks had declared bankruptcy—they didn't have the money to give people.
6. Introduced by President Roosevelt, it helped to establish Social Security, unemployment insurance, and disability insurance.
7. *Answers will vary.* Students may respond that people had no food, no jobs, no money, and therefore no place to live. Life would have been miserable. People may have looked to family members or even the government for help.
8. The New Deal, unemployment and disability insurance, and World War II helped to end The Great Depression.

**Page 15: Comprehension Check: Migrant Workers of California**
1. livelihood—something that provides an income to live on, especially paid work; mecca—an important center for a particular activity; migrant—someone who moves from place to place; squalor—shabbiness and dirtiness resulting from poverty or neglect; semblance—a trace amount of something; sullenness—hostility or bad temper marked by silence
2. The promise of work, since the west was believed to be the new agricultural center of the United States
3. Someone who moves from job to job, living wherever he can so that he can work and provide for his family.
4. *Answers will vary.* Students may describe the homelessness and poverty, the deplorable living conditions and the competition for jobs.
5. The first quotes are used to show special terms. Just below halfway down the paragraph, they show a direct quote from a report from the National Labor Board in 1934.
6. Government camps, including necessary facilities; relief money and food
7. There were so many people looking for jobs, including those who were already living and working in California—often, immigrants. They had to get up early and

make themselves available for work, then wait to see if they were picked for the job. The average was 25 cents an hour, but they were often paid less for their work. They often worked only a few hours, and then had to try to find more work that day.
8. Jobs working on government buildings and transportation systems, or projects in the arts, media, and literacy.

**Page 16: Standards Focus: Elements of Fiction Activity**
*Predictions will vary.*

**Pages 23-24: Anticipation/Reaction Activity**
*Answers will vary.*

**Page 27: Chapter One: Note-Taking and Summarizing**
*Answers will vary.*

**Page 28: Chapter One: Comprehension Check**
1. George is described as "small and quick, dark of face with restless eyes and sharp, strong features. Every part of him was defined: small, strong hands, slender arms, a thin and bony nose." Lennie is "a huge man, shapeless of face, with large, pale eyes with wide, sloping shoulders; he walked heavily, dragging his feet." George is smart and quick-witted with a sharp tongue. Lennie is mentally slow, dim-witted, but manipulative.
2. He doesn't want Lennie to get sick from the still water.
3. He likes to pet soft things. It is dead because he probably petted it too hard at some point.
4. To Murray and Ready's—where they will work.
5. Weed
6. *Answers will vary.* Some students may notice the father-son relationship, how George takes care of Lennie. Others may think it is more like a brotherly relationship, since they seem to fight like siblings. Students may realize that Lennie needs to be taken care of, and George is somehow "assigned" to take care of him.
7. keep his mouth shut and not say anything
8. a mouse
9. his Aunt Clara; he kept killing them by petting them too hard
10. George wishes he didn't have to take care of Lennie so he could find himself a girl and do what he wants without having to worry about Lennie.
11. to own a farm with rabbits and other animals; to be on their own
12. they have each other's companionship
13. back to the river where they were camping; they got in trouble before, so George is just making sure Lennie knows what to do if it happens again. It seems George knows that it will happen again.
14. *Answers will vary.* The incident with the ketchup and when Lennie keeps saying that he will go away and live in a cave if George wants him to. Some students may recognize that Lennie is being manipulative to make George feel bad or make George tell Lennie that he does want him around. It shows that George really does like Lennie and even though he says he doesn't, he probably does want him around as a friend and companion.
15. *Answers will vary.* Steinbeck makes the story more realistic with the use of curse words and foul language. This is the way real people talk—especially these types of men when they are not in the company of women. If Steinbeck used different language and did not use the realism of the way these men really talked, the story may still be good, but not as believable, especially since the novel is so dialogue-heavy, like a play.

**Pages 29-31: Standards Focus: Dialogue**
*Answers will vary. Sample answers are given.*
1. Narrative: Lennie tried hiding his treasure, but George pressed on, knowing Lennie was hiding a dead mouse;
Purpose: Reveals their relationship. Lennie is like a child, picking things up and playing with them. This passage shows that George is used to Lennie doing things like this, and immediately the reader begins to wonder why Lennie is so defensive about the mouse. George doesn't seem to have much patience with Lennie.
2. Narrative: George readied Lennie for their encounter with the boss the next day. He has Lennie practice over and over words that would help him remember not to say anything;
Purpose: Lennie forgets things; George has to prompt and prepare him like a child. This again shows their relationship and

how George has to take care of Lennie to make sure they don't lose their job.
3. Narrative: Feeling sad and guilty for irritating his best friend, Lennie told George he was only kidding and that he really didn't want any ketchup; Lennie knows when he angers George, and wants to fix what he has done wrong.
Purpose: This passage shows how Lennie manipulates George, even though George is the "smarter" of the two.
4. Narrative: Lennie pleaded with George, asking him to tell the story one more time. Lennie knew the story well, but loved to hear it over and over again; they have talked about the plan many times before; Lennie still gets excited about the story, like it was the first time he has heard it.
Purpose: Lennie gets excited hearing about their dream. This is also the first time the reader hears about their dream together.
5. Steinbeck creates the feeling of realism by having the characters speak as they would—curse words and derogatory words and all. Students may realize that the story may not be as believable if the characters did not speak this way. It would not be as interesting if the characters were not like real people—flaws and all.
6. Students may feel as if the banning is good—that the word "nigger" should not be used. They may also have no problem with the language being used, noting that they and their friends speak similarly with no problem, therefore the book should not be banned.
7. Some students may agree that profanity is a part of the realism, giving the book some "spice" and making the book better because of it. Other students may be offended by the use of vulgarities, stating that a book would be just as good or better without the obscenities.

**Pages 32-36: Assessment Preparation: Word Analysis**
*Original sentences will vary.*
1. base: juncture; prefix: none; suffix: -s
   a. noun; a point of connection; joining place
   b. plural noun; points of union; connections
   c. *On one side of the river the golden foothill slopes curve up to the strong and rocky Gabilan mountains, but on the valley side the water is lined with trees—willows fresh and green with every spring, carrying in their lower leaf <u>junctures</u> the debris of the winter's flooding; and sycamores with mottled, white, recumbent limbs and branches that arch over the pool.*
   d. *Sentence will vary.*
2. base: debris; prefix: none; suffix: none
   a. noun; fragments of something broken into pieces
   b. noun; fragments of something broken into pieces
   c. *On one side of the river the golden foothill slopes curve up to the strong and rocky Gabilan mountains, but on the valley side the water is lined with trees—willows fresh and green with every spring, carrying in their lower leaf junctures the <u>debris</u> of the winter's flooding; and sycamores with mottled, white, recumbent limbs and branches that arch over the pool.*
   d. *Sentence will vary.*
3. base: mottle; prefix: none; suffix: -d
   a. verb; mark something with different colors
   b. adj.; spotted; marked with different colors
   c. *On one side of the river the golden foothill slopes curve up to the strong and rocky Gabilan mountains, but on the valley side the water is lined with trees—willows fresh and green with every spring, carrying in their lower leaf junctures the debris of the winter's flooding; and sycamores with <u>mottled</u>, white, recumbent limbs and branches that arch over the pool.*
   d. *Sentence will vary.*
4. base: recumbent; prefix: none; suffix: none
   a. adj.; lying back; in a resting or leaning position
   b. adj.; lying back; in a resting or leaning position
   c. *On one side of the river the golden foothill slopes curve up to the strong and rocky Gabilan mountains, but on the valley side the water is lined with trees—willows fresh and green with every spring, carrying in their lower leaf junctures the debris of the winter's flooding; and sycamores with mottled, white, <u>recumbent</u> limbs and branches that arch over the pool.*
   d. *Sentence will vary.*

5. base: lumber; prefix: none; suffix: -ed
   a. verb; move clumsily
   b. verb; moved clumsily
   c. Lennie <u>lumbered</u> to his feet and disappeared in the brush.
   d. *Sentence will vary.*
6. base: brusque; prefix: none; suffix: -ly
   a. adj.; abrupt or curt in manner or speech
   b. adv.; in an abrupt or curt manner
   c. *"Awright," he said brusquely.*
   d. *Sentence will vary.*
7. base: pantomime; prefix: none; suffix: none
   a. noun; copy; imitation of someone else's mannerisms
   b. noun; copy; imitation of someone else's mannerisms
   c. *But Lennie made an elaborate <u>pantomime</u> of innocence.*
   d. *Sentence will vary.*
8. base: contemplate; prefix: none; suffix: -ed
   a. verb; to think about something as a possible course of action
   b. verb; thought deeply about
   c. *Lennie hesitated, backed away, looked wildly at the brush line as though he <u>contemplated</u> running for his freedom.*
   d. *Sentence will vary.*
9. base: imperious; prefix: none; suffix: -ly
   a. adj.; haughty; dictatorial; overbearing
   b. adv.; in a haughty, dictatorial, or overbearing manner
   c. *George's hand remained outstretched <u>imperiously</u>.*
   d. *Sentence will vary.*
10. base: anguish; prefix: none; suffix: -ed
    a. noun; extreme anxiety; verb; feel or cause somebody distress
    b. adj.; showing exteme anxiety or torment; distressed
    c. *He looked across the fire at Lennie's <u>anguished</u> face, and then he looked ashamedly at the flames.*
    d. *Sentence will vary.*
11. base: yammer; prefix: none; suffix: -ed
    a. verb; talk loudly and at length
    b. verb; howled or wailed as if in pain
    c. *Up the hill from the river a coyote <u>yammered</u>, and a dog answered from the other side of the stream.*
    d. *Sentence will vary.*

**Page 37: Chapter Two: Note-Taking and Summarizing**
*Answers will vary.*

**Page 38: Chapter Two: Comprehension Check**
1. a can of lice repellent; he assumes the man before him had "pants rabbits"; they live in squalor—poor and unsanitary conditions where many people live while they work there
2. George is speaking for Lennie and says they are cousins; he doesn't want any trouble because they have such a unique relationship—the men don't understand a man taking care of another man like George takes care of Lennie; *answers will vary*
3. he is a "little guy" who likes to start fights with "big guys"; he's handy; a lightweight boxer; recently married. He wears a glove full of Vaseline to keep his hand soft for his new wife
4. she's "purty" but she's "got the eye" for other men besides her husband—she's trouble
5. he can tell that Curley is trouble and knows he can rope Lennie into a fight; to return to the place they spent the night (next to the river)
6. he feels that there is going to be trouble—he doesn't like it there
7. that they shoot it and replace it with one of Slim's new puppies; *answers will vary*
8. *Drawings will vary.*

**Page 40: Standards Focus: Analyzing Poetry**
1. a. sympathetic
2. arwy: 1) not in the proper position, 2) not in keeping with plans or expectations; *Answers will vary.* Even the best plans might not go as expected.
3. d. Even the most well-constructed plans can fail.
4. *Answers will vary.*
5. *Answers will vary.* Students may realize that the story may be a tragedy, not ending well for the characters.
6. *Answers are personal and will vary.*

**Pages 41-42: Assessment Preparation: Context Clues**
1. mollified
   a. adj.
   b. *Answers will vary.*
   c. soothed, appeased; calmed

2. pugnacious
   a. adj.
   b. *Answers will vary.*
   c. Belligerent or aggressive in nature; quarrelsome
3. gingerly
   a. adv.
   b. *Answers will vary.*
   c. very carefully
4. handy
   a. adj.
   b. *Answers will vary.*
   c. clever and useful
5. ominously
   a. adv.
   b. *Answers will vary.*
   c. in a threatening way, indicating something bad is going to happen
6. slough
   a. verb
   b. *Answers will vary.*
   c. to cast something off; shed
7. derogatory
   a. adj.
   b. *Answers will vary.*
   c. critical or disparaging
8. flounced
   a. verb
   b. *Answers will vary.*
   c. moved in an exaggerated or angry way
9. plaintively
   a. adv.
   b. *Answers will vary.*
   c. in a sorrowful or melancholy way; mournfully
10. decisive
    a. adj.
    b. *Answers will vary.*
    c. able to make decisions quickly; firm
11. complacently
    a. adv.
    b. *Answers will vary.*
    c. with self-satisfaction; smugly

### Page 43: Chapter Three: Note-Taking and Summarizing
*Answers will vary.*

### Page 44: Chapter Three: Comprehension Check
1. He finds it strange that two men would hang out all the time, taking care of each other like Lennie and George do. George explains that he and Lennie were both born in Auburn and he knew his Aunt Clara. When his Aunt Clara died, George began to take care of Lennie.
2. He realized how gullible and helpless Lennie really was. George is really a nice guy who cares about Lennie deep down inside, even though he always says he would do better without him.
3. She probably thought that because Lennie wanted to pet her dress, he was going to hurt her.
4. George trusts Slim. Also, it helps George make a connection with someone other than Lennie and helps Slim understand that Lennie may be a big guy, but doesn't have bad intentions.
5. George may be afraid that Lennie will accidentally hurt the puppy like he hurt the mice he carried.
6. By visiting whore houses, drinking, and playing cards.
7. Candy has money from his accident and he offers to help pay for the farm. George immediately assumes Candy is making fun of them. George then decides to allow Candy in on the plan. He realizes they could use the money and it would help make their dream come true.
8. He hurt his hand working.
9. He is still thinking about the possibility of having a farm and getting to tend the rabbits.
10. It was his dog—he says he should have done it himself.
11. Lennie crushes Curley's hand
12. He makes him agree to tell people that his hand was crushed in a machine and not by Lennie. He doesn't want Lennie to get in trouble, especially since it was Curley who started the fight. Slim is an honorable man who seeks to do the right thing.
13. He is old and seen as useless and expendable. He probably sees it as symbolic of them getting rid of him, since he is also old and useless.

### Page 45: Standards Focus: Recognizing Vivid Details
*Underlining will vary.*
1. d. sight and sound
2. b. chronological order (the order in which the events occurred)
3. c. anxiety
4. b. The men do not know what to say or do.
5. *Answers will vary.* Student answer may include that Steinbeck wanted to establish

the setting and the tension and anxiety surrounding the shooting of Candy's dog.
6. d. sight and taste
7. b. optimistic
8. *Answers will vary.* Student answer may include that they want to live on a farm, that they would kill their animals to make their own bacon, ham, and sausage, canning their own tomatoes, and making their own cream.
9. d. sight and sound
10. c. tension
11. *Answers will vary.* Student answer may include that the short choppy, sentences help to create a feeling of tension. The short sentences make it sound as if the action is happening quickly and that things are out of control.

**Pages 47-49: Assessment Preparation: Word Origins**
*Inferences and sentences will vary. Dictionary definitions are given.*
1. derision: noun; mocking scorn; ridicule
2. lynch: verb; to seize and punish someone believed to have committed a crime
3. concealing: verb; putting or keeping someone or something out of sight; hiding
4. stride: noun; a long step
5. gnawing: verb; persistent and troubling
6. entranced: verb; in a state of fascination or wonder
7. bemused: adj.; caused somebody to be confused or puzzled
8. cowering: verb; cringing or moving backward defensively in fear
9. regarded: verb; thought carefully about someone or something; judged
10. wryly: adv.; in an amusing and ironic way
11. solemnly: adv.; in a humorless or formal manner

**Page 50: Chapter Four: Note-Taking and Summarizing**
*Answers will vary.*

**Page 51: Chapter Four: Comprehension Check**
1. He has lots of possessions throughout his bunk house. He is alone and secluded because he is black. His room is swept and kept fairly neat.
2. goes to look for his puppy
3. He is immediately defensive of his space. He isn't allowed in the other mens' bunk house, so he doesn't like anyone in his, bothering him.
4. He was born in California on a chicken ranch. He grew up in a white neighborhood and had white friends, although his father didn't like it.
5. He realizes how gullible and naïve Lennie is. He is teasing him to see how far he can go.
6. Although he acts as if he is burdened by their visit, he seems to appreciate the company. He seems very lonely, and seems to welcome the visitors, although he is quite guarded.
7. He says he has heard it all before. He has known other men who have talked about their dream, but never made it a reality.
8. She says she could have "been somebody" and been an actress in movies.
9. She says that she could get him "strung up a tree" for talking to her.
10. *Answers may vary.* Sample answers may include that he felt embarrassed about being pulled into the idea, or that he realizes it could never happen, so he'd rather not get his hopes up.

**Pages 52-53: Standards Focus: Conflict and Effect**
*Answers may vary. Sample answers are given.*
1. man versus himself; Lennie doesn't know his own strength and because of this he keeps killing things.
2. man versus man; George blames Lennie for his problems; he wishes that he didn't have to take care of Lennie all the time so he could do what he wanted. George is resentful of Lennie, which causes him to be hostile towards him.
3. man versus society; Because of the Great Depression, finding work is difficult, and George and Lennie must work to survive.
4. man versus himself; Curley has issues with his size and is insecure with himself, therefore, he picks fights to try to show that he is just as strong as the "big guys." (May be viewed as "man vs. man" by some)
5. man versus himself; Curley is insecure and jealous. His wife is lonely and wants attention because Curley is not giving it to her.
6. man versus society; Because he is African-American, Crooks is not allowed to hang out with the white men in their house. This is a societal issue.

**Page 54-55: Assessment Preparation: Word Roots**
*Connections will vary. This activity may be difficult for some students. Accept all reasonable responses. Sample student answers are given.*

1.
   a. crestfallen
   b. adj.; downcast, disappointed, or humiliated
   c. A tuft is the growth of hair on an animal's head. Connection possibly comes from the idea that an animal's head drops when it has been defeated in a fight.
2.
   a. meager
   b. adj.; unsatisfactorily small; unsatisfying
   c. Emaciate means waste away while meager is something that has been wasted away to a small size.
3.
   a. averted
   b. verb; turned away
   c. Both are related to the idea of turning away from or against something.
4.
   a. disarming
   b. adj.; charming; friendly or trusting
   c. someone who is friendly will act without weapons.
5.
   a. brutally
   b. adv.; in an unrelentingly harsh or cruel way
   c. One who is a brute acts in a brutal way.
6.
   a. scornful
   b. adj.; feeling or expressing great contempt for someone or something
   c. To be scornful is to act with scorn or contempt.
7.
   a. liniment
   b. noun; a pain-relieving cream or ointment
   c. Liniment can be a sticky substance resembling lime.
8.
   a. aloof
   b. adj.; uninvolved with people or events; remote
   c. One who is aloof does not show all sides of themselves.
9.
   a. fawning
   b. adj.; attempting to please with flattery
   c. Both have to do with pleasing. By being fain, one is being pleasant.
10.
   a. appraised
   b. verb; looked over; made a judgment about
   c. To appraise something is to think over or consider.
11.
   a. indignation
   b. noun; anger about an unfairness or wrongdoing
   c. By expressing indignation, one is acting worthy of praise as a decent person.

**Page 57: Chapter Five: Note-Taking and Summarizing**
*Answers will vary.*

**Page 58: Chapter Five: Comprehension Check**
1. Lennie accidentally bounced him too hard and probably broke his neck.
2. He is mad because it wasn't as little as a mouse, so he thought he could play harder with it. Again, he doesn't know his own strength.
3. He has been warned to stay away from her—he knows she's trouble.
4. She is lonely and wants to make a connection with someone. She says she's lonely and never has anyone to talk to.
5. They are in a competition playing horseshoes.
6. She wanted to get away from home.
7. While he was petting her hair, she began to scream. He got mad because she was being too loud and would get him in trouble. He tries to keep her quiet and ends up breaking her neck.
8. George had told Lennie where to go if he got in trouble when they first got to the ranch.
9. Candy
10. George wants to make sure that the men don't think that George had anything to do with her death.
11. He realizes that this will end their dream of having the farm
12. He thinks Lennie took it.
13. shoot him in the gut

14. He realizes that the hope and dreams he had for a short while are all gone. For a while he believed there was hope, which changed his outlook.

**Pages 59-61: Standards Focus: Characterization and Character Types**
*Direct and indirect quotes will vary. Sample student answers are given.*

Lennie
   **Direct Characterization**: "…a huge man, shapeless of face, with large, pale eyes, with wide, sloping shoulders; and he walked heavily, dragging his feet a little, the way a bear drags his paws. His arms did not swing at his sides, but hung loosely." (page 4)
   **Indirect Characterization**: George says about Lennie: "Jus' tell Lennie what to do an' he'll do it if it don't take no figuring. He can't think of nothing to do himself, but he sure can take orders." (page 39)
   **Inference**: George is proud of Lennie, even though he is mentally slow. George takes pride in the fact that Lennie is such an asset because he is so strong and simple.
   **Protagonist; Round; Dynamic**

Candy
   **Direct Characterization:** "He pointed with his right arm, and out of the sleeve came a round stick-like wrist, but no hand." (page 19)
   **Indirect Characterization:** Candy says about himself: "I ain't much good with on'y one hand. I lost my hand right here on this ranch. That's why they give me a job swampin'. An' they give me two hundred an' fifty dollars 'cause I los' my hand." (page 58)
   **Inference:** Candy is old and relatively useless. He is just kept on the farm to do odd jobs, and even he knows how useless he really is. He would like some purpose in his life.
   **Other; Round; Dynamic**

Curley
   **Direct Characterization:** "…a thin young man with a brown face, with brown eyes and a head of tightly curled hair." (page 25)
   **Indirect Characterization:** Candy says about Curley: "That's the boss's son….Curley's pretty handy. He done quite a bit in the ring. He's a lightweight, and he's handy." (page 26)
   **Inference:** Curley is important on the ranch. Candy respects and seems to fear him because of his boxing ability.
   **Antagonist; Round; Static**

Slim
   **Direct Characterization:** "A tall man stood in the doorway. He held a crushed Stetson hat under his arm while he combed his long, black, damp hair straight back." (page 33)
   **Indirect Characterization:** Candy says about Slim: "Slim's a jerkline skinner. Hell of a nice fella. Slim don't need to wear no high-heeled boots on a grain team." (page 28)
   **Inference:** Slim is well-respected on the ranch. He is a man to be reckoned with, and clearly Candy reveres him.
   **Protagonist, Round, Dynamic**

Crooks
   **Direct Characterization:** "Crooks could leave his things about, and being a stable buck and a cripple, he was more permanent than the other men, and he had accumulated more possessions than he could carry on his back." (page 65)
   **Indirect Characterization:** Candy says about Crooks: "Nice fella, too. Got a crooked back where a horse kicked him. The boss gives him hell when he's mad. But the stable buck don't give a damn about that. He reads a lot. Got books in his room." (page 20)
   **Inference:** Crooks is very much to himself—a loner who entertains himself. The guys like him, but he is treated differently because he's black.
   **Other, Round, Static**

Curley's Wife
   **Direct Characterization:** "She had full, rouged lips and wide-spaced eyes, heavily made up. Her fingernails were red. Her hair hung in little rolled clusters, like sausages. She wore a cotton house dress and red mules, on the insteps of which were little bouquets of red ostrich feathers." (page 31)
   **Indirect Characterization:** George says sarcastically about Curley's wife: "Yeah, and she's sure hidin' it. Curley got his work ahead of him. Bet she'd clear out for twenty bucks."
   **Inference:** George is unimpressed by Curley's wife and thinks that she'd leave Curley in a second, given the chance.
   **Antagonist, Round, Static**

**Pages 62-64: Assessment Preparation: Determining Parts of Speech**
1. hurled
   a. subject: he
   b. predicate: picked, hurled
   c. verb
   d. definition: threw something with great force
2. sullenly
   a. subject: he
   b. predicate: looked
   c. adverb
   d. definition: in a hostile, unsociable, or morose way
3. woe
   a. subject: woe
   b. predicate: came
   c. noun
   d. definition: grief or distress resulting from serious misfortune
4. consoled
   a. subject: she
   b. predicate: consoled
   c. verb
   d. definition: provided comfort to someone who is distressed or saddened
5. contorted
   a. subject: face
   b. predicate: was
   c. adjective
   d. definition: greatly bent out of shape
6. writhed
   a. subject: feet, she, screaming (gerund)
   b. predicate: battered, writhed, came
   c. verb
   d. definition: twisted or squirmed, especially from feelings of pain
7. muffled
   a. subject: feet, she, screaming (gerund)
   b. predicate: battered, writhed, came
   c. adjective
   d. definition: wrapped or padded with material in order to stifle sound
8. bewildered
   a. subject: he
   b. predicate: seemed
   c. adjective
   d. definition: completely confused or puzzled
9. pawed
   a. subject: he
   b. predicate: pawed
   c. verb
   d. definition: struck at repeatedly; touched clumsily
10. cringed
    a. subject: she
    b. predicate: whimpered, cringed, jumped
    c. verb
    d. definition: pulled away in a frightening manner
11. sniveled
    a. subject: he; voice
    b. predicate: sniveled; shook
    c. verb
    d. definition: behaved in a whining or self-pitying way

**Page 65: Chapter Six: Note-Taking and Summarizing**
*Answers will vary.*

**Page 66: Chapter Six: Comprehension Check**
1. the river bank; it is where George and Lennie set up camp at the beginning of the story
2. *Answers will vary.* Student answer may include that he may see her because he feels extremely guilty and knows he did a "bad thing"; he knows he would have disappointed her. They talk about how George would be better off without Lennie, the farm and how Lennie won't be able to tend the rabbits anymore, and how George is going to leave Lennie now.
3. a giant rabbit; he's "gonna beat the hell out of" him
4. When George told Candy he was going to leave so the other men didn't think he had anything to do with Curley's wife's death he went and stole Carlson's luger.
5. to distract him and make him think of good things so that he has good thoughts before he dies
6. *Answers will vary.* Student answer may include that it is a mercy killing and the alternative (being put in jail or being killed by Curley) was worse.
7. As Curley said, he would have shot Lennie "in the gut" or worse—beat him up then shot him.
8. George says that Lennie had a gun and that he had to shoot him before he was shot—it was self-defense. The truth is that Lennie didn't have the gun and George just shot him.
9. *Answers will vary.*
10. *Answers will vary, but should be supported with textual evidence.*

11. Carlson doesn't understand the relationship between Lennie and George and how one man could have such love for another. This relates to the themes of loneliness and friendship.

**Pages 67-68: Standards Focus: Theme**
*Answers are personal will vary. Accept all reasonable responses.*

**Pages 69-71: Assessment Preparation: Determining Parts of Speech**
1. lanced
   a. subject: head and beak, beak, tail
   b. predicate: lanced, plucked, swallowed, waved
   c. verb
   d. definition: pierced with a sharp instrument
2. scudded
   a. subject: leaves
   b. predicate: turned, scudded
   c. verb
   d. definition: moved swiftly and smoothly
3. disapprovingly
   a. subject: she
   b. predicate: stood, put, frowned
   c. adverb
   d. definition: with negative judgment based upon personal standards
4. haunches
   a. subject: it
   b. predicate: sat, waggled, crinkled
   c. verb
   d. definition: hip, buttocks, or upper thigh of an animal
5. retorted
   a. subject: Lennie
   b. predicate: retorted
   c. verb
   d. definition: responded in a witty, angry, or insulting manner
6. belligerently
   a. subject: Lennie
   b. predicate: retorted
   c. adverb
   d. definition: in a hostile, aggressive, or fighting manner
7. woodenly
   a. subject: he
   b. predicate: said
   c. adverb
   d. definition: in an emotionless, unresponsive manner
8. monotonous
   a. subject: voice
   b. predicate: was, had
   c. adjective
   d. definition: uninteresting or boring
9. craftily
   a. subject: Lennie
   b. predicate: said
   c. adverb
   d. definition: in a clever or tricky way
10. triumph
    a. subject: Lennie
    b. predicate: cried
    c. noun
    d. definition: an act or occasion of winning or being victorious
11. dutifully
    a. subject: Lennie
    b. predicate: removed, laid
    c. adverb
    d. definition: in an obedient manner; without protest
12. jarred
    a. subject: Lennie, he
    b. predicate: jarred, settled, lay
    c. verb
    d. definition: shook something abruptly

**Page 72: Quiz: Chapter One**
1. b. California
2. c. Weed
3. d. ketchup
4. d. they have a deep connection and friendship
5. b. tending the rabbits
6. Some students may notice the father-son relationship, how George takes care of Lennie. Others may think it is more like a brotherly relationship, since they seem to fight like siblings. Students may realize that Lennie needs to be taken care of, and George is somehow "assigned" to take care of him. Lennie is mentally slow.
7. Keep his mouth shut and not say anything to the boss or anyone else.
8. They want to own a farm with livestock, rabbits, and be self-sustaining, living on their own.

**Page 73: Vocabulary Quiz: Chapter One**
1. i. points of union; connections
2. c. fragments of something broken into pieces
3. j. spotted; marked with different colors
4. g. lying back; resting or leaning
5. f. in a withdrawn or gloomy way; sadly; thoughtfully
6. h. moved clumsily or heavily

7. a. abruptly, angrily, or bluntly in manner or speech
8. l. an imitation of someone else's mannerisms
9. k. thought deeply about
10. e. in a haughty, dictatorial, or overbearing manner
11. b. with extreme anxiety or torment; distressed
12. d. howled or wailed as if in pain; whimpered

**Page 74: Quiz: Chapter Two**
1. b. irritated and suspicious
2. a. sparse and dim
3. c. Candy
4. d. Curley doesn't like big guys
5. b. lonely and flirtatious
6. d. run to the river
7. c. he would get in a fight with Curley

**Page 75: Vocabulary Quiz: Chapter Two**
1. j. to make fun of; tease
2. e. made to feel better; calmed
3. i. belligerent or aggressive in nature; quarrelsome
4. l. in a careful or cautious manner
5. a. clever and useful
6. c. in a threatening way, indicating something bad is going to happen
7. h. to cast something off; shed
8. b. critical or disparaging
9. f. moved in an exaggerated or angry way
10. d. in a sorrowful or melancholy way; mournfully
11. g. able to make decisions quickly; firm
12. k. with self-satisfaction; smugly

**Page 76: Quiz: Chapter Three**
1. true
2. true
3. false: Lennie touched a girl's dress and she thought he was trying to attack her.
4. false: Carlson shot Candy's dog
5. true
6. true
7. true
8. false: Slim ordered Curley to keep his mouth shut about the fight and tell people that he got his hand caught in a machine.

**Page 77: Vocabulary Quiz: Chapter Three**
1. h. mocking scorn; ridicule
2. l. to seize and punish someone believed to have committed a crime
3. j. putting or keeping someone or something out of sight; hiding
4. a. a long step
5. i. persistent and troubling
6. f. in a state of fascination or wonder
7. d. highly unacceptable; deserving criticism
8. b. caused somebody to be confused or puzzled
9. c. cringing or moving backward defensively in fear
10. k. thought carefully about someone or something; judged
11. g. in an amusing and ironic way
12. e. in a humorless or formal manner

**Page 78: Quiz: Chapter Four**
1. Candy, Crooks, Lennie, Curley's Wife
2. African-American, crippled
3. he was black
4. to the booby hatch
5. owning a farm and being on their own
6. Crooks
7. in pictures (movies)
8. was just joking about wanting to be involved in the farm

**Page 79: Vocabulary Quiz: Chapter Four**
1. l. beat, battered, or tore at a person or animal
2. j. uninvolved with people or events; remote
3. k. unsatisfactorily small; unsatisfying
4. b. a pain-relieving cream or ointment
5. d. attempting to please with flattery
6. e. charming; friendly or trusting
7. f. feeling or expressing great contempt for someone or something
8. g. in an unrelentingly harsh or cruel way
9. c. anger about an unfairness or wrongdoing
10. i. turned away
11. h. looked over; made a judgment about
12. a. downcast, disappointed, or humiliated

**Page 80: Quiz: Chapters Five and Six**
1. e. saw a gigantic rabbit
2. f. "I ain't mad. I never been mad, an' I ain't now. That's a thing I want ya to know."
3. b. "You done it, di'n't you? I s'pose you're glad. Ever'body knowed you'd mess things up."
4. g. "You hadda, George. I swear you hadda."
5. c. thought Lennie stole his Luger
6. d. "I'm gonna shoot the guts outta that big bastard myself, even if I only got one hand."

7. a. "Why can't I talk to you? I never get to talk to nobody. I get awful lonely."
8. h. "I seen it over and over—a guy talkin' to another guy and it don't make no difference if he don't hear or understand."

### Page 81: Vocabulary Quiz: Chapters Five and Six
1. h. shouting or laughing at someone in a mocking or hurtful way
2. j. threw something with great force
3. b. in a hostile, unsociable, or morose way
4. e. grief or distress resulting from serious misfortune
5. f. provided comfort to someone who is distressed or saddened
6. d. greatly bent out of shape
7. k. twisted or squirmed, especially from pain
8. l. padded with material in order to stifle sound
9. c. completely confused or puzzled
10. i. struck at repeatedly; touched clumsily
11. g. pulled away in a frightened manner
12. a. behaved in a whining or self-pitying way
13. i. pierced with a sharp instrument
14. h. moved swiftly and smoothly
15. b. with negative judgment based upon personal standards
16. c. hip, buttocks, or upper thigh of an animal
17. j. responded in a witty, angry, or insulting manner
18. e. in a hostile, aggressive, or fighting manner
19. f. in an emotionless, unresponsive manner
20. l. uninteresting or boring
21. d. in a clever or tricky way
22. a. an act or occasion of winning or being victorious
23. g. in an obedient manner; without protest
24. k. shook something abruptly

### Page 82: Vocabulary Review: Chapters 1-3

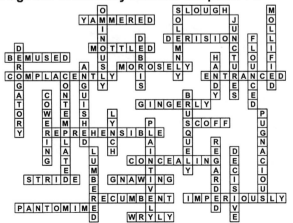

### Page 82: Vocabulary Review: Chapters 1-3

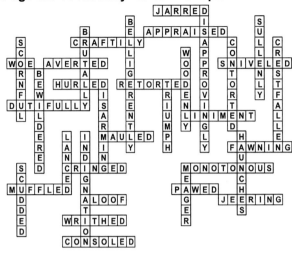

### Page 84-86: Final Test
**Part A**
1. e. "Why do you got to get killed? You ain't so little as mice."
2. h. "I ain't mad. I never been mad, an' I ain't now."
3. i. "You hadda, George. I swear you hadda."
4. f. suspicious of George's intentions
5. d. tells Lennie that he will go to the "booby hatch"
6. a. the first one to join Lennie and George's dream
7. b. a welterweight fighter
8. g. "Well, I ain't giving you no trouble. Think I don't like to talk to somebody ever' once in a while?"
9. c. owned a Luger pistol

**Part B**
10. b. California
11. c. Weed
12. d. ketchup
13. d. They have a deep connection and friendship.
14. b. tending the rabbits
15. b. irritated and suspicious
16. a. sparse and dim
17. c. Candy
18. d. Curley doesn't like big guys
19. b. lonely and flirtatious
20. d. run to the river
21. b. Lennie petted a girl's dress
22. c. Carlson
23. b. Crooks
24. d. George
25. c. is segregated because of his race
26. d. all of the above
27. d. all of the above

28. c. The Great Depression
29. c. makeshift towns of very poor people
30. c. Franklin Roosevelt

**Part C**
31. *Answers will vary.* The incident with the ketchup and when Lennie kept saying that he would go away and live in a cave if George wanted him to. Some students may recognize that Lennie was being manipulative to make George feel bad or so George would tell Lennie that he does want him around. It shows that George really does like Lennie and even though he says he doesn't, he probably does want him around as a friend and companion.
32. *Answers will vary.* Steinbeck makes the story more realistic with the use of curse words and foul language. This is the way real people talk—especially these types of men when they are not in the company of women. If Steinbeck used different language and did not use the realism of the way these men really talked, the story may still be good, but not as believable, especially since the novel is so dialogue-heavy, like a play.
33. *Answers will vary.* Students may notice the fact that Lennie liked to pet mice, but petted them too hard and broke their necks; Lennie petted the girl's dress in Weed; Lennie killed the puppy by playing too hard with it.
34. *Answers will vary. Accept all reasonable and supported responses.*
35. *Answers will vary. Accept all reasonable and supported responses.*

**Pages 87-89: Final Test: Vocabulary**
**Chapters One and Two**
1. c. points of union; connections
2. h. fragments of something broken into pieces
3. g. spotted; marked with different colors
4. f. moved clumsily or heavily
5. i. abruptly, angrily, or bluntly in manner or speech
6. a. an imitation of someone else's mannerisms
7. e. thought deeply about
8. b. with extreme anxiety or torment; distressed
9. d. howled or wailed as if in pain; whimpered
10. q. to make fun of; tease
11. m. belligerent or aggressive in nature; quarrelsome
12. j. in a careful or cautious manner
13. r. clever and useful
14. k. in a threatening way, indicating something bad is going to happen
15. o. to cast something off; shed
16. p. critical or disparaging
17. l. in a sorrowful or melancholy way; mournfully
18. n. able to make decisions quickly; firm

**Chapters Three and Four**
19. b. mocking scorn; ridicule
20. c. to seize and punish someone believed to have committed a crime
21. i. putting or keeping someone or something out of sight; hiding
22. a. a long step
23. h. persistent and troubling
24. f. in a state of fascination or wonder
25. g. highly unacceptable; deserving criticism
26. d. caused somebody to be confused or puzzled
27. e. cringing or moving backward defensively in fear
28. n. in a humorless or formal manner
29. l. beat, battered, or tore at a person or animal
30. q. uninvolved with people or events; remote
31. p. unsatisfactorily small; unsatisfying
32. j. in an unrelentingly harsh or cruel way
33. m. anger about an unfairness or wrongdoing
34. r. turned away
35. k. looked over; made a judgment about
36. o. downcast, disappointed, or humiliated

**Chapters Five and Six**
37. h. shouting or laughing at someone in a mocking or hurtful way
38. f. threw something with great force
39. e. grief or distress resulting from serious misfortune
40. i. provided comfort to someone who is distressed or saddened
41. d. greatly bent out of shape
42. g. twisted or squirmed, especially from pain
43. b. padded with material in order to stifle sound
44. c. completely confused or puzzled
45. a. pulled away in a frightened manner
46. p. behaved in a whining or self-pitying way
47. j. pierced with a sharp instrument
48. m. responded in a witty, angry, or insulting manner
49. k. in a hostile, aggressive, or fighting manner

50. r. uninteresting or boring
51. l. in a clever or tricky way
52. q. an act or occasion of winning or being victorious
53. o. in an obedient manner; without protest
54. n. shook something abruptly

**Pages 90-92: Final Test: Multiple Choice**
**Part A**
1. a. Crooks
2. b. Candy
3. d. Curley
4. c. Carlson
5. c. Lennie
6. b. Curley's Wife
7. a. George
8. d. Slim
9. b. George
10. a. Crooks
11. c. California
12. b. Weed
13. d. ketchup
14. d. They have a deep connection and friendship.
15. c. tending the rabbits
16. c. irritated and suspicious
17. a. sparse and dim
18. b. Candy
19. d. Curley didn't like big guys
20. b. lonely and flirtatious
21. d. run to the river
22. c. Lennie petted a girl's dress
23. c. Crooks
24. d. George
25. b. is segregated because of his race
26. d. all of the above
27. d. all of the above
28. b. The Great Depression
29. a. makeshift towns of very poor people
30. b. Franklin Roosevelt

**Part B**
31. *Answers will vary.* The incident with the ketchup and when Lennie kept saying that he would go away and live in a cave if George wanted him to. Some students may recognize that Lennie was being manipulative to make George feel bad or so George would tell Lennie that he does want him around. It shows that George really does like Lennie and even though he says he doesn't, he probably does want him around as a friend and companion.
32. *Answers will vary.* Steinbeck makes the story more realistic with the use of curse words and foul language. This is the way real people talk—especially these types of men when they are not in the company of women. If Steinbeck used different language and did not use the realism of the way these men really talked, the story may still be good, but not as believable, especially since the novel is so dialogue-heavy, like a play.
33. *Answers will vary.* Students may notice the fact that Lennie liked to pet mice, but petted them too hard and broke their necks; Lennie petted the girl's dress in Weed; Lennie killed the puppy by playing too hard with it.
34. *Answers will vary. Accept all reasonable and supported responses.*
35. *Answers will vary. Accept all reasonable and supported responses.*